Playing With Fire

Playing With Fire

the use and abuse of music

by

Alex Robertson

BARRATT MINISTRIES PUBLICATIONS

Manchester M14 5QH, England

PLAYING WITH FIRE - THE USE AND ABUSE OF MUSIC

by **Alex Robertson**

British Library Cataloguing-in-Publication Data

A catalogue record for this book is available from the British Library

ISBN: 0 9528222 0 2

Published 1996 by **Barratt Ministries Publications**
114 Daisy Bank Road, Victoria Park,
Manchester M14 5QH, England.

Printed by **Gazon Uitgeverij,** Den Haag, Holland.

Contents

INTRODUCTION

I made me great works: I builded me houses, I planted me vineyards: I made me gardens and orchards: I gat me servants and maidens ... I gat me men singers and women singers, and the delights of the sons of men, musical instruments, and that of all sorts. So I was great, and increased more than all that were before me in Jerusalem ... and whatsoever mine eyes desired I kept not from them, I witheld not my hand from any joy ... then I looked on all the works that my hand had wrought, and on the labour that I had laboured to do: and behold, all was vanity and vexation of spirit ...

Ecclesiastes 2:4-11

The 20th Century - A Music Explosion

If an 18th century scientist were to discover the secrets of time travel and drop in on the last decade of the 20th century, I wonder what would amaze him the most? Cars, planes, television, nuclear physics, space travel, computer technology? So much is new! The acceleration of technological development in just the last 100 years is extraordinary. But another equally amazing fact is that, all the way down the line, music has constantly capitalized on these new developments and technologies. Along came radio - and there are now thousands of radio stations devoted almost exclusively to music. Then along came television - and is there nowadays a single TV programme without music in it? Along came the motor car - and most cars now come equipped with stereos or even CD players. Along came computers, and now, lo and behold, music on computer! One thing is clear from all this - music is of crucial importance to society today.

Our 18th century time traveller would surely be amazed at the abundance of music - in the shops and the supermarkets, in restaurants and swimming baths, in the car and even in the pocket. What would he make of the sophisticated stacks of music-producing machinery adorning the living rooms of virtually every house? Or all the shops devoted exclusively to music? And if he should chance to go to a pop concert, what would his reaction be to the apparently mesmerizing effect of this incredibly loud music on the audience? Might he not conclude that music had become the new religion and taken over these people's lives? Certainly music has never been so accessible to the masses, so important to people, so indispensable to society as it is today. The advent of the "personal stereo" is one more symptom of people's desire - and often even their need - to have music as their constant companion.

For centuries music has been a major force in society, often at the forefront of current thought and opinion, setting trends and forming ideas which greatly influence man's understanding of himself and the world around him. But now we are faced with an unprecedented explosion of music.

What are we to make of this 20th century phenomenon? One thing is certain - it is vital that we try to understand it. Is it a good thing that music should be so important to us? How has it become so important? What forces have been at work to accomplish this? Where is it all leading us? And where do we stand as Christians?

Hundreds of books have been written on the subject, many from a Christian viewpoint. But many of the most fundamental questions still remain unanswered. For example: What exactly is music? What is actually happening to you as you listen to music? How does it affect you? Why does it affect you? Then there are moral questions. Is this effect good or bad, or can it be both, or is it neither? Is music in any sense a moral issue or an issue of conscience? As Christians, can we discern any principles which we can confidently say are relevant to our attitude towards music and our use of music? And there are specific questions about scripture and music. What are we to make of the virtual silence of the New Testament concerning music, and how do we reconcile that with the importance given to music in Christianity today? What does the Bible tell us, if anything, about the origins of music?

If we cannot find solid answers to such questions, we cannot have a firm basis for a Christian understanding of music. But if we can find answers - and I believe we can - then we are able to reach clear conclusions, and make decisions about our attitudes and behaviour in this age of the music explosion.

Part I

THE NATURE OF MUSIC

Would'st thou be in a dream, and yet not sleep?
Or wouldest thou in a moment laugh, and weep?
Wouldest thou lose thyself, and catch no harm?
And find thyself again without a charm?

Bunyan, *The Pilgrim's Progress*

There is a mysterious magic about sound. Consciously or unconsciously it is assumed to be the most direct means of expression of gods, spirits, men and even inanimate objects.

René Clemenicic

Chapter 1

The Physical Nature Of Music

The wind blows where it wishes, and you hear the sound of it, but do not know where it comes from, or where it is going ...

John 3:8

What is music? Any scientist can tell you. Or at least, any scientist can give you the scientific answers - that is, the answers that deal with the physical nature of music. Science cannot answer the questions that deal with the spiritual aspects of music. As far as physics is concerned, all sound is simply vibration. Soundwaves are vibrations which travel through suitable materials, and to which human beings and animals may be sensitive. A soundwave, set up by some vibrating source, pushes the molecules of air in front of it; those molecules in turn push the molecules in front of them, and so on. But the soundwave doesn't stop when it hits a solid - for example, the human body. In fact, sound passes through solids more easily than it does through air! So every sound you "hear", whether musical or not, is affecting and vibrating every molecule in your body. If you listen to a very low or very loud sound (a pneumatic drill, or a loud bass note) you can physically feel the vibration inside you.

The Whistle That Killed

When I was a boy I heard a gruesome tale about a scientist who constructed a machine something like a giant referee's whistle. It was built so big as to produce an extremely low "note" with a very strong vibration. When the machine was completed, the intrepid inventor switched it on. In an instant he was dead - his internal organs had been "scrambled". Whether this story is true or not I don't know. But it certainly could happen. The sheer physical power of very low, very loud soundwaves could easily produce vibrations which would be too much for the human body to handle.

The Marshall Space Flight Centre in America has a vibrations test laboratory which contains a machine for generating very high sound pressure levels (SPL's), comparable to the sound level inside a rocket shuttle during launch. A music magazine reported: "To give you an idea of what those SPL's are like, empty coke cans placed in the room will splinter into hundreds of pieces as they are hit with 170 decibels of white noise ... such sound pressure levels could easily kill a person by inducing haemorrhaging."[1]

On a milder level, studies done on air-conditioning systems which produce a low frequency vibration have shown that buildings equipped with some such systems can induce adverse physical effects on the personnel. There is actually a phenomenon known as "Sick Building Syndrome", which causes abnormally high sick-rates among the work-force in affected buildings, and one of its causes has been traced to the physical effects of low-frequency sound from the air-conditioning system.

At the opposite end of the scale, very high sounds above our hearing threshold (known as *ultrasound*) are used in such things as the cleaning and de-greasing of industrial equipment. The vibrations of these ultra-high soundwaves literally shake the dirt off a piece of glass or metal.

The Pleasure Factor

Much has been made of the damage to hearing that can be caused by loud music, for example at rock concerts. Indeed, many musicians, from the classical music field as well as the heavy rock aficionados, suffer from *tinnitus*, an unpleasant ringing noise in the ears, which is a result of damage to the ear caused by exposure to loud music.

Recording engineers also have a reputation for demanding high listening levels in the studio. "Some engineers can never get enough level", says Ben Duncan, himself a recording engineer, writing in *Studio Sound* magazine. Duncan, however, believes that there is another, less well-known reason why people like loud music - the pleasure factor. High volume levels act as a mild drug, giving the listener a "kick" in the form of a pleasure stimulant. "For music above about 95 dB Laeq, there is an adrenaline rush, comparable to the energising effects of amphetamines. If the rush is accompanied by some kind of pleasure, it is all the more likely to become addictive. But the ear-brain combination can soon accommodate the level. So then the rush runs out, and going louder is one natural reaction to get it back again."[2] (To put Duncan's figure of 95 decibels in perspective, levels in heavy rock concerts have been known to peak as high as 140 dB.)

In Chapter 7 we shall be looking at further aspects of music's similarity to a drug, including some of its psychological effects and moral implications. But for now we are concerned with a purely physical effect, one which the majority of people (and virtually all rock and pop music fans) will have experienced. Ben Duncan summarizes: "Working in a high SPL soundfield involves being empowered with a naturally occurring amphetamine substitute." Volume-crazy recording engineers have in the past often simply been labelled as hard of hearing, but their behaviour should be understood afresh, he contends. "Instead of being some sign of acute deafness, it is actually no more than another variant on human addiction-to-pleasure." The association between drugs and rock music becomes more obvious, as does the more recent connection of rave music with the drug Ecstasy, when we consider that the volume level of the music is also acting as a drug - it is just one more factor in the pleasure trip.

Deaf Musicians

You may be surprised to learn that there are professional musicians who are completely deaf. Their ears are entirely dysfunctional. All of their recognition of sound comes from sensitivity to vibrations. Of course, the human ear is an unbelievably sensitive instrument. The membrane of the ear drum can pick up a sound with an intensity of 0.000000000001 watts per square metre. That figure is better grasped by analogy! It is equivalent to the amount of light or heat that would be received in absolute darkness from a 50 watt light bulb at a distance of 3,000 miles! Such is the incredible sensitivity of the ear. But a completely deaf person can play the violin in a symphony orchestra. Think of the sensitivity to vibration alone, without the ear, necessary to play perfectly in time and in tune with 70 other musicians, never mind at exactly the right volume! These are staggering thoughts, and they show just how much we are affected by soundwaves.

You Are What You Hear

We sometimes say that "we are what we eat" because our food is absorbed into our system and becomes "a part of us". In another sense we speak of the influence of words on our way of thinking to make us "who we are". But what of the effect when every molecule in your body is put into a state of vibration by a complex organized mass of soundwaves for long periods of time? That's what music is! Penetrating every fibre of your physical being as well as affecting your mind and emotions, the music literally surrounds and passes through you. At that moment you are, in a sense, what you hear. Moreover, the effects of music don't stop when the soundwaves stop. Music stays in the mind. You can hear an orchestra or a rock band in your head! It stays in the subconscious. Sometimes we can dream music. Perhaps you have experienced waking up with music in your head. Today, because of the mass media, most people "know", or have in their memory, literally thousands of songs or pieces of music. Its effects and influences are, in this sense, permanent.

These are only some of the purely physical effects of music. When we add to these all the emotional, psychological and spiritual influences music can have upon us, it is no wonder it has such captivating power.

Notes

1. *The Mix*, May 1994
2. *Studio Sound and Broadcast Engineering*, June 1995

Chapter 2

The Part We Play - The Use Of Music

In matters of principle, stand like a rock; in matters of taste, swim with the current.

Thomas Jefferson

Is sound a moral issue? Is there such a thing as a good or bad sound? The simple answer is no. A sound in itself is neither good nor evil. The furthest extremes of sound, as we have seen, can be physically dangerous, even fatal. But a C sharp or A flat is neither good nor bad, neither godly nor demonic. This has a simple but important consequence. It means that there is no such a thing as "Christian music" per se. There aren't any Christian chords. Similarly, there is no such thing as the devil's harmony, or the devil's melody.

The Devil In Music?

Medieval church musicians thought differently. They considered, for instance, that the harmonic interval of a diminished 5th (the distance exactly halfway between an octave) was evil, on the basis of its jarring dissonance. They called it "diabolus in musica" (the devil in music), and forbade composers to use it. When they listened to music, they heard some harmonies or combinations of notes which were pleasant to the ear, ("consonant"), and other combinations which were "dissonant", harsh and unpleasant on the ear. So they concluded that the pleasant harmonies were good and the dissonant ones were bad, and because they discerned (rightly) a spiritual quality in music, they decided (wrongly) that the pleasant harmonies were *spiritually* good - godly harmony, if you like -

and the dissonances were spiritually evil - the devil's harmony, or "the devil in music".

Similarly, they regarded the note B as a "taboo" note because of its unusual sound in the context of the modal language which they used: and the mode which corresponded to what we now call the scale of C major was not a preferred "church mode"; it was regarded as fit only for secular or profane music. Interestingly, this type of thought, whereby spiritual qualities are attributed to sounds and notes, has a modern counterpart in New Age music. New Agers regard modal music as more spiritual than tonal music. But the roots of these ideas (often derived from Gnostic philosophy) are actually occultic and based on falsehoods.

Sounds, notes and harmonies are, in themselves, neither good nor evil. However, the way in which music is used can be good or evil. The use of music is very much a moral issue. There is such a thing as the abuse of music. This distinction between sounds in themselves, and the use of those sounds, has other important consequences; and the fact that we are Christians ought to greatly influence the way we use music, whether we are performers or listeners.

Rhythm And "The Devil's Beat"

Up to now I have only made reference to harmony and melody. Rhythm is a rather different consideration. Music is usually described as being made up of the three elements of melody, harmony and rhythm; so we tend to think of these three as being of a similar nature. But rhythm is fundamentally different from melody and harmony. Rhythm is to do with intervals of time, not of pitch or frequency. Moreover, melody and harmony can both exist on their own and be called music. But rhythm on its own is not necessarily music. The regular, repetitive rhythm of a car engine is not music; neither is the rhythm of a heartbeat.

When rhythm is joined to harmony and/or melody, it does constitute an element of music. But it is a rather different element to melody or harmony, and is capable of distinctive effects, some of which can be harmful.

When rhythm is repetitive, regular, upfront and insistent, it can cause physical changes in brainwave patterns and body metabolism, even to the extent of being able to induce a state of trance or hypnosis. Some of the most notorious instances of this occur in connection with pagan religious rituals, where drums are used to deliberately induce a trance state in a witch-doctor, medium or shaman, so that in the "opened-up" trance state they become possessed by a spirit.

It is this sort of effect that has given rise to suspicions of something called "the devil's beat". Such an idea is immediately dismissed by most Christian musicians, and rightly so. But it is possible that the people who talk about the devil's beat may be nearer the truth than we imagine. To point to a particular rhythmic pattern and say "That is the devil's beat", or to look upon all rhythm as being suspect, would be quite wrong. But the use of rhythm to alter mind-states and open the spirit up to demon possession is, to me, an abuse of rhythm, and it marks rhythm out as an element with a particular potential for danger. We do need to exercise care and thoroughly understand the principles which concern the use and abuse of music.

Satanic Samples?

The world of music technology now abounds with "sound modules" (black electronic boxes to the uninitiated!) full of "sampled" sounds; that is, sounds that have been recorded and stored in a digital format, and can be reproduced and manipulated on a synthesizer in a staggering variety of ways. Let's suppose that one of these "samples" was a recording of a witch doctor playing or singing, or a satanist performing in an occult ritual. Part of an advert for one such sound module runs as follows:

"Imagine playing the Australian didjeridu, a 30,000-year-old instrument whose haunting drone provides a trance-like background for Aborigines during meditational rituals. Or the flowering chime of the Indonesian Gamelan, whose performance is part musical, part mystical communion among players..."[1]

The question is: should a Christian musician be using, or even listening to, those sorts of sounds? I would answer: there's no reason why not, because *it's only sound.* The way it was being used when it was recorded has nothing to do with the inherent physical qualities of that same sound as it exists in the sound module, waiting for you to use it in, hopefully, quite a different way. A sound in itself cannot be possessed by a spirit, any more than the "food offered to idols" referred to by the apostle Paul could be possessed by the evil spirit to whom it was offered. Paul's conclusion on that subject was: "Eat whatever is sold in the market, whether it has been offered to idols or not, and don't let it bother your conscience at all, unless by eating it you are going to offend someone else's conscience" (see 1 Corinthians 8:4-13 and 10:25-33). I believe this same principle applies here. Whatever the origin of the sound sample, there is no need for that to bother your conscience; you may feel free to use it. However, if your conscience is troubled about the origins of the sound, you are better to avoid using it. As Paul says, all things are pure, but if you do something with an uneasy, doubting conscience, not in faith, then that is sin. (See Rom 14:20-23.)

Sounds without life

The New Testament has surprisingly little to say about music. But from what it does say, we can glean some useful truths. Paul, in fact, does seem to lend support to the idea that sounds in themselves are merely physical things, with no spiritual life or meaning of their own, and that it is only the way in which they are used that gives them meaning and value. "Even things without life which produce sound, whether a flute or a harp, if they do not give a distinction in the sounds they make, how will you know what is being played?" (1 Cor 14:7) There has to be a meaning to the sound if it is to be anything more than a lifeless sound from a lifeless instrument. Meaning can only be given to it by a person - the player - and the meaning can only come from the player's expression of his or her spirit.

That would imply that it is the musician, rather than the music itself, that is important; but this is only partly true. The way in which musicians use sounds can create a harmful use, or abuse, of the music itself.

One such abuse has for a long time been at the centre of the Christian debate about rock music - a debate which, so far, seems to have been distinguished only by a miserable lack of any clear, basic principles from which to draw convincing conclusions; the controversy has been fuelled on both sides by authors who are too biased in favour of their own opinions and prejudices to examine the situation objectively. We need to try and take that objective look. But before we explore any examples of "use" and "abuse", we will take a broad overview of some of music's effects, and try to answer a few fundamental questions. How does music affect us, and why does it affect us so powerfully? Are there any inherent "powers" in music? Could they be called "spiritual powers"? Are there styles of music that we should avoid listening to? Are there methods or musical influences that we should avoid when we create our own music? The answers to these questions can help us to see more clearly how we as Christians should regard music, and how we should use it.

Notes

1. Advert for Proteus 3 'World' sound module.

Chapter 3

The Spiritual Nature Of Music

Can a man take fire in his bosom, and his clothes not be burned?

Proverbs 6:27

We have briefly examined some of the ways in which music affects us physically. Of course, music also affects the non-physical part of our nature - not only the body and the brain, but also the mind, the emotions, the spirit.

Does music have any power of its own? Music certainly influences people very powerfully. But the nature of that power is not so easy to define, for there are many different sorts of power, and many different ways of using it. However, there are two analogies that may help us here.

1: Music as a tool

Music can be compared to a tool, which can be used for good or evil - take for example an axe, which could be used to chop wood for a fire to warm people, or to kill someone. But in itself, the axe has no power. Music is the same. In itself, music has no power. It is neutral, a dead thing, possessing only physical, not spiritual, qualities. It only becomes powerful when it is taken up by a person. In other words, the power is in the person.

On the other hand, a person cannot exercise the power without the tool. The axe is necessary for the power to chop wood or to murder.

Music, then, is a tool, neutral in itself, but capable of use or abuse. Sounds in themselves are dead, but when those sounds are organized and used by a spirit, for example a composer or performer, then they take on spiritual power, just as when an axe is thrown it is given energy and power (scientifically termed "kinetic" or moving energy), and then it becomes a powerful thing in itself. So when we talk about the "powers" of music, we are talking not about any inherent power that sounds have in themselves, but of the effects of spirit-to-spirit communication through the medium of sound. This is what we call music: and this is why music has power; that is to say, it is capable of powerful effects.

2: Music as a medium

Music is also a medium for the transmission of a message. I use the word "medium" in the sense of "a means of communication". A message is by nature a spiritual thing; only spirit can give meaning and sense to a message. Music is a medium, a vehicle, a channel for one spirit to transmit a message to another; it is a particularly effective medium, just as copper is a good conductor of electricity. It offers little resistance, allowing the energy to flow easily. In much the same way, when you hear a piece of music that affects you powerfully, what is actually happening is that your spirit is identifying with the spirit of the music. What is "the spirit of the music"? Simply the spirit of the composer and/or the performer of the music. Music is essentially a means of spiritual communication. When you are affected by music, it means the message is getting through, spirit to spirit. Because music is such a transparent medium, we can easily be led to believe that the power belongs inherently to the music itself. But this is not true. The power is spiritual; that means it originated in a personal spirit, and finds its destination in another personal spirit.

I should add that by "spiritual", I do not mean necessarily "godly". The devil is also a spirit; so is every human being. Music of every style and from every origin pays homage to the spiritual aspect of its art, whether in classical music that claims to be inspired by God (or by any other spiritual source), African ritual music used to conjure up spirits, or The Beatles high on drugs and eastern mysticism. Most of the musicians who have reached the top are there because they have realized the key - that music is spiritual.

Music, then, is a tool, a means to an end, a medium for a message, a body for a spirit; and because it is such a finely developed tool and such an excellent medium, there are two basic dangers which immediately become apparent. The first is that, just as the tool can be powerfully used, so it can be powerfully abused. The second is that (to adapt Marshall McLuhan's famous phrase) the medium can easily become the message. The means becomes the end: the importance shifts from the message of the music to the music itself. It becomes "art for art's sake". And there, we see in outline the two basic dangers we face with regard to music: the abuse of spiritual power, and the love of music for its own sake.

A Cautionary Note

Any discussion of the spiritual effects of music is bound to be subjective, and much of my illustration is necessarily from my own experience. I want to share these experiences because I suspect they are actually very common; and if your experience agrees with mine, you may be better able to identify with my understanding of the principles behind the various "powers" I describe.

The very fact that we cannot comprehensively list and analyse these effects, influences and powers should itself give us good reason to treat the music we create and listen to with respect, caution, and, as Christians, with diligent prayer. We are dealing with something we don't know very much about, and something potentially very powerful. We are playing with fire, and we must be careful. It is not enough to say "Music is a wonderful gift of God". Gifts can be abused, and music is no exception. We have been born into the 20th century with a deeply preconditioned understanding of music, and it is so important for us to stand back and, with prayers to God for wisdom, seek to understand the powers we are dealing with and their relation to God.

Evocative Power

One of the most instantly recognizable "powers" or spiritual qualities which can be transmitted through music is evocative power. This is what you might call a power that works by association. I sometimes hear a piece of music which I haven't heard for several years. As I hear it again now, perhaps just at a certain point in the music, it might even be one particular chord, I suddenly experience a vivid "flashback". I can remember exactly the circumstances when I last heard that music, I can remember the people I was with, how they looked at that time; I can remember the place and its sights and sounds and smells and atmosphere; I can even remember my thoughts - and this evocative power is uniquely able to draw out of my memory feelings, attitudes, fears and insecurities from the past. They all suddenly become real to me once more; in one sense I actually relive them. My whole experience seems to be "evoked", entire and complete, by the music.

Of course, music is not the only medium capable of carrying evocative power. Re-reading a long-forgotten book can also have the same effect, as can a visit to an "old haunt". These memories can be evoked through all of the senses. But (and maybe it's just because I'm a musician) to me, music is a more potent vehicle than any of the others.

Chapter 4

An Imaginary Life - A Personal Testimony

The world is for all of us not only what it is; it is what we believe it to be.

A.W.Tozer

Imaginative Power

Imaginative power is closely related to "evocative power", but it is not so much to do with evoking memories of the past, as with the present and the future - the things that could be. I am thinking here particularly about the way in which music can set you dreaming, romanticizing, or fantasizing. I remember once, while I was at university, listening for the first time to a symphony by Mahler on the radio. Throughout the symphony I was looking at a picture in my room, an illustration, as it happened, for Tolkien's fantasy novel "The Lord of the Rings"; a picture full of mysterious mountains and mists, with a sage-like figure in the centre who seemed to have an aura of tremendous wisdom about him, an other-worldly, secret wisdom. The whole scene fascinated me and drew me in - one might almost say it cast a spell on me. And the combination of this visual fantasy with the evocative, heart-stirring sounds that I was hearing, was such that for the whole duration of the symphony I was quite transfixed, and "in another world".

In my university days (before I became a Christian) I was what I would call a "romantic" in the broadest sense of the word - full of dreams and visions and high ideals. In my imagination there was a person I wanted to be, or thought I was, and a world I wanted to be in, or created for myself. But it bore little relation to the truth. Like most "romantics", I had precious little practical application of my great ideals, and still less sense of reality, and God had to do a very thorough and painful work to extricate me from this deceptive fantasy and bring me, kicking and protesting, into the real world.

I don't think my state was particularly unusual. People didn't think I was weird or reclusive. They might have said I was quiet, and happy with my own company, but not withdrawn or introspective. Neither was I a habitual daydreamer; I was quite diligent, and I lived a fairly normal, practical existence. I make that point because I think that many "normal" people live in something similar to the fantasy world I have described, and that music, and the way that they use it, contributes to the construction of this fantasy. The purpose of the fantasy may be as a defence or a rebellion against reality, or it may have no purpose at all, but purely be a product of personality and circumstance. But it is not reality. Christianity is reality, and if we are living in fantasy, that can be a great hindrance to our Christian life. Our fantasy conflicts with reality, colouring the truth with falsehood and making it impossible to see the truth.

Descriptive Power

I have sometimes wondered whether my involvement with music was to blame for my evolving this sense of fantasy. Or was it the other way round - that having these romantic, imaginative leanings already in my personality, I found in music something which fed and nurtured those fantasies? Whatever the case, music can certainly be a potent vehicle for the powers that move and fuel the imagination. Is this a good thing? Not necessarily. It wasn't for me at university. But that was at least partly because of my personal attitude.

What about the music itself? Can that be dangerous? Let's look at an example of a piece of music specifically designed to play on the imaginative power of the listener.

The classical composer Smetana wrote a symphonic poem which is a musical description of the course of the River Vltava in Czechoslovakia from its source as a mountain stream, through rapids and fields and finally, in its broad grandeur, through the city of Prague. Smetana's skilled, descriptive imagery is surely entirely wholesome and legitimate. How could such pleasant music be in any way harmful?

I believe this can only be a personal matter for the listener to decide. Though the composer intended no abuse, it is still possible for the listener to misuse the music. For me in my university days it might well have had a harmful effect. Whatever Smetana's intended "message", I could have created a fantasy out of it, and fantasy in this sense (something that draws you away from reality and traps you inside your own mind) is wrong. I would call it a matter of conscience; I'd have to decide personally for myself whether it would be beneficial or harmful for me to listen to that music; whether its result would be detrimental to my sense of reality, or whether no harm would be done.

Two Opposing Worlds

As it happens, I did have to make many such "decisions of conscience" when I became a Christian. It was clear to me then that I was being confronted for the first time in my life by *reality*, the reality of God's Spirit living in me and working in me; a reality I could for the first time express (instead of having to hunt around in music and relationships and a thousand other things for experiences with which to impress myself). I became keenly aware of the vast difference between this reality and the fantasy world I had previously inhabited, and of the relationship between this fantasy and music - particularly certain pieces of music which seemed to draw me straight into that fantasy world. Here again I can't distinguish between types or styles of music to say that one is more powerful than another. Something from the pop charts might seem particularly powerful to me, but so might (for instance) a 19th century symphony, or some religious music from the 1500's. But I did find that for a long time I was quite unable to listen to certain pieces of music. If I tried to listen to them, to "test the water", as it were, I would be immediately plunged back into a sea of memories, imaginations, and that other fantasy realm which I was so thankful to have left.

However, these days I find I can listen to almost any music without feeling the "pull". *Almost*. There is still music that "does the wrong thing" for me. I suspect that in these few remaining cases I am dealing with something more than just my own personality. I think here that probably the music itself is to blame. My suspicion is that in these instances I am responding to the spirit of the composer - that there was something of this fantasy world in the composer's own mind and intention when he was inspired to write, something of the same imaginary, unreal nature - and that I have "tuned in" to his spirit. That, after all, is what every composer wants you to do; but if you tune in to music that came from a warped or depraved mind, from a manic depressive or a drug addict, then you can expect some of that spirit to be transmitted to you.

The Wagner Addicts

When I was at music college some of my fellow students would from time to time stock up with food and shut themselves in a room to listen to "The Ring" (a series of four very long operas by Wagner, full of mysterious, awe-inspiring, mystical Germanic legend and folklore). Such behaviour was the subject of some mirth amongst those at the music college who did not share these students' enthusiasm for Wagner; but nevertheless their self-imposed confinement was not deemed to be particularly unusual. It is quite normal and acceptable for musicians to be fantasists. A composer like Wagner undoubtedly encourages such fantasy in his music; and his mind was certainly depraved. (See chapter 10 for more on Wagner.) When the intention of a piece of music is to draw you away from reality and trap you in a world of fantasy, that is an abuse of music, and an abuse of the human mind.

Finally, it is important to say here that *imagination and fantasy are not the same thing*. For a study on the positive use of imaginative power, and on the difference between imagination and fantasy, see Chapter 26.

Chapter 5

Expression And Impression

It is tragic how few people ever 'possess their souls' before they die. 'Nothing is more rare in any man', says Emerson, 'than an act of his own.' It is quite true. Most people are other people. Their thoughts are someone else's opinions, their lives a mimicry, their passions a quotation.

Oscar Wilde

Expressive Power

Music is a marvellous vehicle for human expression. Expression is a spiritual power, because when I express myself, it is essentially my spirit that I express. As a Christian I often find that when I want to express myself to God, words alone cannot do justice to what I feel inside. This is where music really excels. When words are not enough, I can sing, or play an instrument. And I have often heard some of my fellow Christian musicians express themselves spontaneously through their instruments in a most powerful and moving way. When this happens I find, interestingly enough, that it has exactly the opposite effect from that of the "imaginative" power of music; instead of tending towards fantasy and unreality, it seems to speak like a revelation from God, and makes reality clearer and more real. There is a freshness and a life about it, which I think can only be put down to the active, gracious presence of God's Spirit in the life of that musician at that time. The expression of God's Spirit is, I believe, one of the supreme purposes of music. In as much as we can distinguish "use" and "abuse", the ability to express God's Spirit through music must rank high among the "uses".

Getting Into A State

Expression, of course, has an opposite. If I define expression as the use of music *to convey my own experience* to others, then impression - the opposite - is the use of music (or anything else) to affect me by *changing my own experience*, altering my mood or state of consciousness, or to give me some sort of a "trip" or "high". These are all different ways of saying the same basic thing: I am listening to the music because I want to have an experience that is different from my present experience.

You will realise from this that "impression" is what I was experiencing during the episodes I described earlier in connection with "evocative" and "imaginative" powers. The whole purpose of the music, as far as I was concerned, was to give me an experience which was different from my own reality. It had nothing whatever to do with expression. Expression is always a reflection of your own reality.

Interestingly, as a performer of classical music, I was regarded by my audiences as someone who expressed himself with some success. But actually, my life was not really conducive to expressing anything! I didn't have anything in me to say. However, this is not an important issue in classical music. A classical musician is trained to be not so much a voice for himself, as a voice for someone else - the composer. And I, if you like, listened to the music as I was playing it, and expressed what I was hearing - *expressed what I was being impressed by.* Classical musicians are often taught that their role is to be nothing more than a vehicle - just as music is a vehicle for the spirit, so the performer is a vehicle for the music, the next link in the chain. Spiritually, it is a passive role. What classical musicians are not taught is that the opposite is also true: the composer and his music can also be a vehicle for you - you can actively express yourself through someone else's music, if that music ties in with what you feel and what you want to say. I had to discover this for myself after my Christian life had begun.

Music and Hypocrisy

Before I became a Christian I was for several years a member of a string quartet, and our collective behaviour and attitudes showed up another striking anomaly. When we played in concerts, we played musically together, in harmony, in unity. But as people, we were often not in unity at all! Sometimes there was outright hostility between us. In the rehearsals we might be shouting at each other, frustrated that we couldn't get our own way, or going through personality clashes; and occasionally in concerts we might not even be on speaking terms! And yet in the music we seemed to "express" harmony, unity, joy, peace... Of course, the audiences loved it, as it represented to them the height of culture and civilization - because to many people, music (especially classical music) is nothing less than a means of salvation for mankind, embodying the hope that the noble element in mankind will triumph in the end, and all things will turn out for good in a world of peace and beauty. We were the ambassadors of this hope! The audiences clapped, delighted at our performance, and said how wonderful it must be to be four people in such marvellous unity, making beautiful music together. But we couldn't have been more hypocritical ambassadors if we'd tried!

Chapter 6

Manipulative Power - Their Lives In Your Hands

Power undirected by high purpose spells calamity.

Theodore Roosevelt

Manipulative power is the ability of skilled musicians to influence or control their audience's emotions, minds and spirits. As is the case with most of the other powers we are discussing, manipulative power is not a bad thing in itself, but it is quite obviously open to abuse. Some musicians have a thorough understanding of the techniques and methods by which power can be generated and unleashed. Others don't understand it, but just learn by experience "what works". Either way, music is an ideal medium for manipulative power. In fact, all the "powers" we have discussed so far are influences which manipulate or change the listener's experience - but here the manipulative power is very much in the hands of the musician, because he or she is the one who decides what is used, when, and why.

This has a particular application to worship music, praise, and any other type of music used in church which involves the congregation. The days of the monopoly of the church organ are over, and there was not much the organist could do to sweep the congregation off their feet - except perhaps to turn the volume up full and step on the lowest note available! But now there is such a variety of expressive instruments and wonderful sounds that the limitations are gone: and the better the musicians, the more power is in their hands.

As someone who has been involved in "worship groups" of various sorts for several years, and having a thorough musical training behind me, I have learned how to "get a congregation going". To put it bluntly, I don't need God's presence to be there for me to be able to get people clapping, standing up, and praising God at the top of their voices. All I need is a careful use of volume and rhythmic development, coupled with the appropriate harmonies and key changes at the right moment, some nice "full" keyboard sounds, and a good rhythm section to back me up. The same is true of quiet worship songs. Setting up an "atmosphere" is not difficult at all, with the array of beautiful sounds now available on most synthesizer keyboards.

This is what I mean by the manipulative power of music. That's quite some power in your hands. Some musicians are good at this sort of thing (for better or worse), and some aren't. Some understand what they're doing, and others don't. They're "just doing it". But it is important to understand, because if you realise the implications of what you're doing, you might not be inclined to carry on doing it in the same way - or even doing it at all! In Chapter 14 we shall explore further some of the implications of the use of manipulative power in worship music.

Chapter 7

Music As A Drug

The abuse of a harmless thing is the essence of sin.

A.W.Tozer

Many of the things we use in life as "tools" or mediums for a message seem to carry an addictive potential of their own. Indeed, the similarity between music and a drug is striking. A drug such as heroin can be "used" or "abused". In itself, heroin is just a plant; as such it is morally neutral. God created it. But in its use, it has moral implications - it can be used positively as a painkiller in medicine, but if it is used with the purpose of giving you a "drug trip", then that is, from a Christian point of view, morally wrong - it is an abuse of the body and the mind, resulting in physical and mental addiction. It becomes a vice which traps people and enslaves them.

Music, too, can be abused. For all its positive qualities, music is also capable of doing damage, wreaking havoc with a person's psyche, and tearing open the psychological and spiritual safeguards put into our nature by God to protect us from danger to the health and balance of our minds and spirits.

Jimi Hendrix, the rock guitarist (now passed into legend as the father of "acid rock" or drug-influenced rock) once made a revealing statement - revealing because it showed up the purpose and philosophy behind his music. "Music is spiritual", he said, "You can hypnotize people with the music, and then when you get them at their weakest point, you can preach into their subconscious what you want to say".[1] In a similar vein, rock singer Dave Crosby once declared that he could "steal kids from their parents" by getting into their minds through the music and changing their value systems. That, he noted, "removes them from their parents' world very effectively".[2] What powers are at work to accomplish this? One of them is famous as the hot issue at the centre of the rock music controversy - hypnotic or mesmeric power. The big question is: can music have a hypnotic effect? Jimi Hendrix seemed to be convinced that his music could. But pinning down the nature of the hypnotic experience is not easy. The principles that are involved here need careful examination.

Hypnosis - Anaesthetizing The Brain

Mesmeric or hypnotic power is the only power out of all those we have considered which is in itself an abuse. The others are not; there is nothing essentially wrong with things that are evocative, or that draw on the imaginative powers of the listener - Jesus' parables do that. Any problems arising from those "neutral" powers are to do with the way in which they are used. But mesmeric power is different. Human beings were never meant to be hypnotized. Although the nature of hypnosis is not fully understood by medical science, there is no doubt that the hypnotic state does exist, and can be induced.

Hypnosis can be achieved through many different techniques, amongst which are those that focus the mind on something which is strictly regular, repetitive and insistent. The classic example is the hypnotist's "swinging watch"; when it becomes the focus of attention to the exclusion of everything else, it induces an altered state of mind by effectively shutting down or switching off a part of the brain. Another notorious instance is the "Chinese water torture", the sound of a dripping tap, again regular and insistent, and heard in otherwise total silence. African tribal drumming rituals seem to perform the same function; in fact it is often their deliberate intention to induce a state of trance by the use of rhythm, in this case more complex than the simple "rhythm" of the watch or tap, but equally insistent, regular and repetitive. The consistent volume level also adds to the mesmeric effect. It performs the purpose Jimi Hendrix referred to - it "opens people up".

Hendrix's hypnosis seems to work by effectively anaesthetizing part of the brain's normal functions of awareness. The ordinary functioning of the brain includes a kind of physical "defence mechanism," a natural device to protect the spirit. This protection is an important part of God's design, and ensures that my spirit is always under my control - the way God intended. If I want to open myself up to someone, I do it by my choice. I choose to let the barriers down. But what appears to happen with hypnotism is that this defence is anaesthetised, taken out of action, and control is subconsciously surrendered to another power. What Jimi Hendrix "preached", once his music had broken down people's defences and "opened them up", went straight into their spirits. They had handed over the control of their spirits to him, whether they knew it or not. Very probably only a few of them knew that this was what they were doing. As far as they were concerned, they were just "freaking out" and "letting go".

Rock Music In the 90's

So what about rock music today? Can people really be hypnotized by a drum beat? A heavy rock beat is certainly loud, and insistent, and repetitive, and regular. But it is not isolated. There is some variety added to the sound from vocals and from other instruments in the band. So whatever hypnotic effect there is ought to be lessened by these factors. On the other hand, the effect could well be heightened by the consistently loud volume, and the rhythm is a major part of that volume. Constant high volume works as effectively as constant silence as a backdrop to the mesmeric power of insistent rhythm, and the disorienting effects of spotlights and strobes may also contribute to the influence.

It is certainly not the case that rock music is always hypnotic, or that rock necessarily has any harmful effect. It is very much a matter of the degree or intensity both of the music and of your involvement and concentration. Nevertheless, considering the ethos of the rock style, the purpose behind it, and the reasons why it evolved in the way it did, certain questions demand answering. Why is so much volume necessary? Why did the rock beat become so heavy? There must be a reason.

In Chapter 9 we will go on further to examine "the roots of rock". But first let us consider the principle by taking a more general look at the roots of style - why new musical styles emerge and develop, and what they mean.

Notes

1. *Life magazine*, 3rd October 1969
2. *The Rolling Stone Interviews*, Vol. 1, p. 410

Chapter 8

Spirit And Style

'We'll wait awhile,' the master said, 'that thus
Our senses may grow used to this foul stench
And after that, it will not trouble us.'

Dante, *Inferno*, Canto IX

New musical styles do not come about by accident. Behind the evolution of any style, there lies a spirit, a purpose, a philosophy. History teaches us that as a musical style develops, it usually moves from a radical "fringe" origin into the mainstream of popular music, and in doing so it invariably loses some of its initial power; yet its founding purpose remains the same. *Jazz*, for example, was born out of the desire for free expression, and this is reflected in its use of improvisation. Often it was the same sort of "free expression" that led men through the doors of a brothel. (Early jazz was commonly identified with "brothel music"; in fact, the word "jass" was black slang for sexual intercourse around the turn of the century in New Orleans. "Boogie-woogie" has similarly unfortunate origins - it used to be a common colloquialism for syphilis.) *Country music* carries the ethos of the simple, down-to-earth "country boy" who loves the free things in life and has no time for the rat-race of the city. Its use of simple harmonies and rhythms, and its links with folk music, are a musical reflection of that root philosophy.

The ethos of *classical music*, evolving out of the strict confines of church music, always retained something of the desire to strive towards spiritual heights - with or without God. With the arrival of the humanistic Renaissance in the 15th century, and even more so in the 18th century "Age of

Enlightenment," when man became "the measure of all things", classical music came to represent all that was noblest and best in mankind, the height of culture and civilization. This philosophy has many consequences: for instance, there is still an association in many people's minds between classical music and cultural snobbery. Others, as we have already seen, look to classical music as a hope for mankind, almost a means of salvation, believing that if man can live up to his best, the good in him will somehow triumph over his lower nature and all will be well. Diverse as classical music is, it has always appealed to people who think they have "refined sensibilities".

These little "cameos" of different styles are, of course, gross generalizations, but my point here is not to try and analyse their origins in depth, but rather to show the way in which the development of a style is basically linked to the philosophy and spirit which gave birth to the style. In essence, a style evolves because someone wants to say something particular, and they create music that fits what they want to say. Style is the servant of spirit.

The Acceptance Of The New

All the main musical styles in existence today have moved into the mainstream of culture only after a radical beginning "on the fringe", and in their origins, the fierce power and strength of the spirit behind the style is always most apparent. But alongside the changes in the style itself runs another most interesting trend. The style may "calm down" or become more "middle of the road", perhaps in order to appeal to a wider audience; but at the same time, the reactions and attitudes of the public to the original "fringe" style also undergo drastic changes. This can be clearly seen in the case of classical music through the centuries. The works of many famous composers were initially greeted with outrage. I have on my bookshelf a "Lexicon of Musical Invective", which consists of contemporary press reviews of the premières of works by composers from Beethoven to Bartók. Every single review is highly derogatory! Here is an example of a review which appeared in a Viennese newspaper in 1806:

"Recently there was given the overture to Beethoven's opera *Fidelio*, and all impartial musicians and music lovers were in perfect agreement that never was anything as incoherent, shrill, chaotic and ear-splitting produced in music. The most piercing dissonances clash in a really atrocious harmony, and a few puny ideas only increase its disagreeable and deafening effect."[1]

Such reviews were far from being the rantings of a lone reactionary; they were invariably the general consensus of cultural opinion at the time. Yet these very same works, which were at first universally condemned, now belong to the mainstream of high culture, universally accepted as among the most beautiful music in the world. Attitudes change! Why? *Because we get conditioned.* We grow to accept and take for granted what was initially outrageous. Maybe we can put some of the initial hostility down to the human trait of "non-acceptance of the unfamiliar". Samuel Butler commented that "the only things we really hate are unfamiliar things". But I think there is more to it than that. I think that behind the sense of outrage that characterizes popular reaction to new styles, is a genuine intuitive sense that something is wrong. The same sense of outrage among the general public accompanied the first chart entries of The Beatles in the early '60s. What to us today sounds harmless or nice, sounded wrong, disturbing, horrible and scandalous to the people who first heard it. These were not prudish people, just ordinary people.

That really should make us think. It is difficult, in fact almost impossible, for us to objectively measure how much we are conditioned to accept what we hear. All we can do is guess, by looking at examples like these "unconditioned reactions" to Beethoven and The Beatles, what the truth really is. Who is right, and who is wrong? Is there a strange, inbuilt philistinism in us that will not at first accept what is beautiful, but rejects it as worthless? Or is our initial reaction right - is there a jarring in our spirit, in every human spirit, as we recognize that something has entered the world which is disturbing and "wrong"? And if so, what is it that we are sensing is wrong? Is it something that ordinary people, who may be living lives that are far from godly, nevertheless recognise as somcthing ungodly, another step further away from God and from reality, something which is going to further the cause of the kingdom of "the prince of this world"?

That may sound fanciful and rather pessimistic. But I believe that a progressive trend away from God can be traced in human civilization, and that scripture recognises this trend. We will examine this in more detail in Part II.

These are emotive issues, and we must try to be objective in our analysis and assessments. We can so easily cloud the issue with personal feelings about the music we like or hold dear. My purpose is not to give conclusive answers, but to pose the question, which is this: Is the instinctive distaste or disgust of the listener to "new music" actually the instinctive truth? And does that truth then gradually get drowned, as the power of the spirit behind the style begins to work its charms (for those powers, as we have seen, are many, and subtle, and do not generally tend towards God and truth)? Can we compare these first hearings to, for example, the first experience of a cigarette, which invariably causes a fit of choking and coughing along with feelings of distaste, revulsion, even nausea - yet swiftly begins to do its addictive work, whereupon the smoker, initially repulsed, is now hooked, and craves the thing that at first was so abhorrent to him?

Notes

1. Quoted in Nicolas Slonimsky, *Lexicon of Musical Invective* (Washington, 1969) p. 42

Chapter 9

The Roots Of Rock

Rebellion is as the sin of witchcraft.
1 Samuel 15:23

What is the purpose, the reason, the spirit, behind the rock music style?

"Rock" is now a widely accepted style, and the term covers everything from overtly satanic heavy metal to sophisticated, mainstream "adult rock", mild, refined and middle of the road. But this is rock music thirty years on from its initial explosion in the '60s. Then it was a different matter, socially speaking.

I suppose few people would doubt that rebellion was a foundational spirit behind the evolution of rock music. (This isn't only true of the origins of rock. Some aspects of other styles, including jazz and classical music, were also formed in the crucible of a fiercely independent and subversive spirit). But with the beginnings of rock it is particularly obvious. Please note what I'm saying here. Firstly, I'm not talking about people's attitudes to rock music (Christian or otherwise) today. I'm talking about its origins. Secondly, I'm not blaming rock music for rebellion, as some people do. But I am blaming rebellion for rock music! A whole generation, sick of the society their forefathers had created, was bent on revolution, and bent on breaking free of the restrictive and hypocritical morals imposed on them by their parents. The explosive force of that generation's reaction is still felt today. Nothing was too extreme to explore, nothing was "out of bounds": any means which provided some new experience, whether drugs, music, sex or black magic, was O.K. It was part of the spirit of the times. "Freak-outs" were part and parcel of this violent search for experience. The music was deliberately designed to create an atmosphere in which to get utterly involved, body, mind and spirit, and lose sense of anything else. The motto of that generation was "Let go, freak out, and see what happens". We have to remember just how extreme the "cutting edge" of the '60s revolution was, because that's where we can see the roots and purpose of rock, the reason why it was created, the spirit behind the style.

The Testimony Of The Rock Heroes

No-one is better informed to tell us about that than the people who were at the heart of it. John Lennon has spoken about some of the experiences that inspired his creative output. As a teenager, Lennon said that he "used to literally trance out into Alpha" (an altered state of consciousness) "... seeing these hallucinatory images."[1] Talking of his songwriting process, he said: "It's like being possessed; like a psychic or a medium."[2] Does that give you any more pause for thought about the general public's initial reaction to The Beatles?

Jim Morrison, lead singer with The Doors, was described by his biographers as "an obsessed disciple of darkness, who rejected authority in any form, the explorer who probed the bounds of reality to see what would happen."[3] Morrison typified, in extreme form, the philosophy of that generation, and his music was directly related to and derived from that philosophy.

Ray Manzarek, keyboard player with The Doors, gives an insight into the band's acquaintance with drugs, sorcery and "altered states". Having described the ritual in which a Siberian shaman (witchdoctor) enters a trance, to the pounding of drums for hour upon hour, Manzarek went on: "It was the same way with The Doors when we played in concert. The sets didn't last that long, but I think our drug experiences helped us to get into it that much quicker ... It was like Jim (Morrison) was an 'electric shaman' ... the band would keep pounding, and little by little it would take him over".[4] Note the clear evidence there of deliberately used hypnotic techniques. Certainly any effect, hypnotic or otherwise, which might induce a changed state of consciousness, or some new experience that "probed the bounds of reality", was welcomed and pursued, simply because it was new, different, rebellious and outrageous.

Christian attitudes towards rock music have always been polarized. People either love it, and vigorously defend it, or hate it, and aggressively attack it. Whichever side they are on, they seem to take it personally. It's an emotive issue, because people identify personally with the music. One thing is clear, however. The morals and values of the '60s were not Christian values. They were the values of the permissive society, of rebellion against authority and against Christianity. This much is well documented. My aim is not to leap in with a statement for or against rock music, but to try and highlight the principles and issues which will enable you to make up your own mind. Thus far, my point is to draw attention to the link between musical style and the spirit which gives birth to the style. Style is rooted in spirit. Of course, this has practical consequences. If you are into heavy rock, (regardless of whether it's labelled "Christian" or not), and if you would say that you're not inspired by rebellion and you don't want to get into the sort of "new experiences" that John Lennon and Jim Morrison spoke of - then you have to ask yourself why you want to use a style that was originally created with that purpose? What is your purpose in using high volume, distorted sounds or screaming vocals? Why do you need them? If you don't need them, why do you use them? Why do you like them? These aren't meant to be loaded questions. You have to reach your own conclusions. I'm not giving dogmatic answers; I'm just posing questions, and suggesting that you need to answer them.

Notes

1. *The Playboy Interviews with John Lennon and Yoko Ono* (Berkeley, 1982) p. 169
2. *ibid.*, p. 203
3. Jerry Hopkins and Daniel Sugerman, *No One Here Gets Out Alive* (Warner Books, 1980), back cover
4. *ibid.*, pp. 158-160

Chapter 10

A Classic Delusion

There are moments when one is more ashamed of what is called culture than anyone can be of ignorance.

Edward V. Lucas

The common consensus of cultural opinion in the world today is that without the works of Bach, Mozart, Beethoven, Tchaikovsky and the other great composers, mankind would be spiritually impoverished. Classical music is held in high esteem, even in reverence, by society. No other type of music has been so consistently identified with spirituality and even godliness. How has this come about?

Culture And The Church

Until the 18th century, a good deal of what we would call classical music was church music, designed for use in worship. Even in Mozart's day, a good deal of music was religious. Composers wrote "sacred works" for choirs and orchestras, masses, oratorios, motets and the like. But gradually, as the influence of the church declined, secular music took prominence, and today even religious works are now usually performed in a secular context, i.e. in a concert hall rather than as part of a church service. In the last few centuries, concert halls and theatres tended to be shunned by evangelicals because of their associations with worldliness, non-christian and even anti-christian activity. But today, culture is becoming an important feature of evangelical Christianity (notably, so is political action, and a desire to be influential in the commercial and scientific world. The significance of that will become apparent when we examine "the origins of culture" in Chapter 12). Rather than viewing this as a case of the values of the world invading the church, one school of thought suggests that Christians are reclaiming a heritage that really always belonged to them. Classical music, in their view, is rooted in godliness (or, as it is often more vaguely termed, "spirituality"), and classical composers are the inheritors and perpetuators of that spirituality.

Spirituality Or Christianity?

The American Christian music company "Word" recently published a book with the intriguing title, "The Spiritual Lives of Great Composers". Written by an evangelical Christian, Patrick Kavanaugh, its aim is to highlight the "deep spirituality" of many composers' lives, the implication being that the inspiration for their music was godly, and that Christians should embrace classical culture as a part of their "spiritual heritage". A "recommended listening" list is offered to encourage Christians to listen to more classical music.

In one sense, all the book does is encourage and affirm a cultural status quo. Music-lovers are encouraged to keep on being music-lovers, and new converts to culture are enthusiastically sought. Aficionados of classical music and culture have always done this sort of thing. But now it is being done in the name of Christianity, and there is a new twist to the old theme. Immersion in classical culture is identified with spirituality, and spirituality is in turn identified with godliness. The implication is that you can't go wrong by getting to know and love classical music, and that it can only help, strengthen and deepen your own Christianity. Nowhere in the book is there any suggestion that music can become an idol, never a hint that it could be a kind of substitute spirituality, a subtle and seductive rival to

Christianity. Indeed, the book gives no indication that such a possibility has even crossed the mind of the author; he comes across, in fact, as a man sold out to music. That is not unusual; in my experience the majority of Christian musicians are in willing submission to the power of music - I might almost say "under the spell". Music holds a magic for them that they cannot - or will not - let go.

Despite Patrick Kavanaugh's protestations that "so much has been written about the negative side of composers' lives", the fact is that most people are unaware of any of the details of composers' lives. What people are aware of is the almost mythical status of classical music; they know it ranks amongst mankind's greatest and most exalted achievements, and the general impression most people have of composers is of the "spiritual", noble, brilliant genius blessed with a "great gift". "Great" thus becomes identified with "godly". But that is a very dangerous identification. Likewise, beauty becomes associated with goodness, but this too, though a commonly held view, is a short-sighted generalization.

Many of the great composers were, at least nominally, Christians. But the undoubted "spirituality" of their music is not necessarily anything to do with Christianity. Most of the classical composers lived in an age where Christianity was the established religion, to which virtually everyone adhered, at least in name. It was part of the accepted social structure. But we can hardly deduce from this that the classical composers were all true Christians. In fact, for many people, Christianity was nothing more than a nominal social convention. Frequently their religion was mixed with superstition, blending elements of Christianity with the common philosophies of the day, and this made for a strange, incongruous, contradictory mix: Christianity and humanism, Christianity and Freemasonry, Christianity and Aryanism, Christianity and pantheism. By quoting selectively from the writings and correspondence of some classical composers, I think I could probably persuade you that they were genuinely Christian. But in most cases, I could just as easily compile an alternative selection of quotes which would convince you that these same men were anything but Christians!

What are we to believe, then? As it happens, that is not a difficult question to answer. It's easy to claim to be a Christian and to talk about God; but talk means nothing; by themselves "beliefs" are only empty words. Jesus explained that people are known by their fruits - by their lifestyles, attitudes, and actions, the things that grow out of true faith. However, the fruits of the lives of many composers include quite a few shocks!

Christian Composers

There are, to be sure, composers who have had a genuine Christian faith. Bach seems to stand out as a man whose life and words testified without contradiction that God was important to him. A similar sincerity of faith has been ascribed to Vivaldi, Handel, Haydn, Mendelssohn and Dvorak. There is evidence in their writings that they had a genuine devotion to God. However, they were certainly also devoted to music. Music was their life. We cannot read their minds and hearts; we do not know their motives. But we can all surely identify with the danger that all Christian music-lovers face, even when we are dealing with the best and most wholesome music - the danger of idolatry, of loving the music more than God. God demands our sole allegiance; He will not share His lordship of our lives with any rivals, and sooner or later every Christian musician is faced with this conflict. It is a personal confrontation with God, a test for each one of us. Some pass the test and yield to God: others are unable - or unwilling - to release their hold on music, and live the remainder of their lives trying to serve two masters. Whether these composers passed or failed the test we do not know - although perhaps we might expect to read in their diaries or letters some account of this kind of confrontation and conflict. But we never do.

The remainder of this chapter explores the spiritual qualities of some great composers' lives. However, we should bear in mind that this is only one side of the story. Our motives and attitudes in listening to their works are also decisive factors. As listeners we always have to contend with the danger described by Paul in his letter to the Romans: "worshipping the creation instead of the Creator" (Rom 1:25). Nobody has expressed it better than C.S.Lewis: "Every poet and musician and artist, but for grace, is drawn away from love of the thing he tells, to love of the telling, till down in Deep Hell, they cannot be interested in God at all but only in what they say about him".[1]

Music is a means of worshipping God, expressing ourselves to God and "telling" about God. But we can so easily move from love of God to love of the music which tells about Him, until we are only interested in music - in art for art's sake.

"You Shall Know Them By Their Fruits"

The aforementioned composers are those who seem to stand most firmly at the Christian end of the spectrum. Even amongst them, there are curious traits. For instance, although Mendelssohn was a Lutheran, he inclined towards Catholicism at one point in his life, but his passionate love of the music of Bach (a Protestant) anchored him to Lutheranism.[2] Was it love of God or love of Bach that had the most effect on Mendelssohn?

However, when we turn our attention to other great figures in classical music, the picture becomes more disturbing. I only have space for brief comments about each composer, and of course, there are many more important names than those mentioned here; but this is a reasonably representative cross-section. I make no apology for deliberately highlighting the more questionable aspects of these composers' lives and works, because it is these aspects that will affect our attitudes towards them.

Beethoven's crude manners left people aghast. Once, when he was brought the wrong order in a restaurant, he promptly hurled the dish full of food into the waiter's face. He was so unkempt that on another occasion he was mistaken for a tramp, arrested, and dumped in the local jail, before someone came and identified him as the great composer. What Patrick Kavanaugh calls his "untraditional faith" included the fact that, though born a Catholic, he "never practised this faith" and "avoided going to church", but "had a strong interest in eastern literature, and he even copied three Hindu passages which he kept under glass in his desk ... he had no scruples whatsoever in quoting pagan verse..."[3]

Schubert was also a Catholic who, towards the end of his short life of 31 years, was "led astray" by a friend: "Few details remain of their escapades in the Vienna nightlife, but most scholars today believe Schubert contracted syphilis as a result".[4]

Berlioz abandoned Christianity early and became openly hostile towards it, ridiculing the beliefs of his fellow composer Mendelssohn. Berlioz' religion was basically pantheism. He had no time for the Christian God: "God, standing aloof in his infinite unconcern, is revolting and absurd". His God was Shakespeare, to whom he wrote a kind of "prayer": "Thou alone for the souls of artists art the living and loving God!"[5] Berlioz believed passionately in the power of music, and he asserted that when music's powers are fully concentrated on all of man's faculties (brain, mind, heart, ears, nerves) "then it is acting in its proper realm ... then it is that we are gods".[6] He was an early experimenter with drugs, and probably took opium for the first time in 1829, before writing his "Symphonie Fantastique", which is a musical picture of a disturbing scenario dreamed up by Berlioz himself. The "program" for the symphony runs as follows: A young musician of morbid disposition and powerful imagination takes opium and is plunged into a deep sleep ... He dreams of his beloved, who periodically appears before him, each time bringing a sense of foreboding ... The fourth movement is entitled "March to the Scaffold": he dreams he has killed his lover, is sentenced to death, and "witnesses his own execution". In the final movement, "he sees himself at a witches' Sabbath, in the midst of a ghastly crowd of spirits, sorcerers and monsters of every kind, assembled for his own funeral". Then his murdered beloved appears, "mingling with the devilish orgy", and the music ends with a "ludicrous parody of the *Dies Irae*" ("Day of Wrath", part of the latin Catholic funeral service) musically combined with the witches' Sabbath Dance.

Liszt was an extraordinary example of self-delusion. Kavanaugh comments, somewhat euphemistically, "it is particularly difficult to reconcile his devout spirituality with his outrageous lifestyle".[7] In fact, it is impossible! While Liszt believed himself to be "a fervent Christian all his life", he was "an incorrigible womaniser who careered from one glamorous affair to another ... Liszt led a life of epic sensual self-indulgence". He fathered several illegitimate children, and carried on his whole life in the same fashion, showing no signs of repentance, "flirting with his students while in his seventies, yet maintaining throughout his life that he was a "true believer".[8]

Tchaikovsky was thought until a few years ago to have died of cholera. Now it appears that his death was connected with his homosexual activity. The respected Russian scholar Alexandra Orlova uncovered evidence that Tchaikovsky committed suicide at the behest of a court of honour which had met to assess the implications of Tchaikovsky's alleged sexual relationship with a male member of the Russian Imperial family.[9]

Wagner's spiritual life must rank among the most disturbing of any composer. Though he claimed to be a Christian, morals did not seem to worry him. He "ignited a roaring scandal by wooing ... the wife of Hans von Bulow, a noted conductor and devotee of Wagner's music. The von Bulows' marriage was annulled conveniently..."[10] An unashamed hedonist, he loved to be surrounded by satins and silks, and owned a collection of over forty silk dressing gowns. His composition study at Munich was festooned with satins in soft pastel colours. He could not bear the feel of coarse fabric, and all hard, straight lines were eliminated from the room. Aided by "soft perfumes", he gained his musical inspiration from stroking the luxurious fabric of his specially upholstered couch. Wagner certainly had an interest in spiritual things. One of his pieces was entitled "The Love Feast of the Twelve Apostles". Utterly convinced of the music's godly qualities, he wrote of its first performance, "the Holy Ghost was poured out ... we were all transported".[11] Bold words indeed! But the Jesus that Wagner believed in was actually very different from the Jesus Christians know. Wagner, an anti-semite, could not bring himself to believe that Christ was a Jew; instead he believed that Jesus was born "among the silent vegetarian communities founded by Pythagoras".[12]

Wagner and Nazi Ideology

Patrick Kavanaugh approvingly quotes Wagner's belief that Christ's blood was "a fountainhead of pity which streams through the human species". But he does not point out that Wagner believed Christ's blood to be "a higher fluid ... a godlike manifestation of the highest qualities of the Aryan spirit". Wagner believed in the superiority of the Aryan race over other races, including the Jews. Hence his anti-semitic stance. Exactly the same belief led Hitler to kill six million Jews. Wagner's music is suffused with these beliefs; to take just one example, he believed that the Aryan race was descended from the hero-gods Siegfried and Hercules: Siegfried appears as the hero of Wagner's huge opera-cycle "The Ring". Christ's blood, according to Wagner, "wiped away the sin of racial decline and redeemed inferior breeds".[13]

"Wagner rejected the Old Testament ... dismisses the Ten Commandments", admits Kavanaugh.[14] He wrote to his friend and admirer King Ludwig of Bavaria, "the Jewish race is the born enemy of pure humanity and of all that is noble in it". "In 'Know Thyself', Wagner spells out the cause of mankind's degeneration - the Jews - and he hints at the only hope for its regeneration - elimination of the Jews".[15] Wagner's beliefs formed such an important basis for Nazism that Hitler himself once said, "In order to understand National Socialist Germany, one must know Wagner".[16] Incredibly, despite these repulsive and clearly anti-christian doctrines, Kavanaugh comments on Wagner's "intense spiritual life" and wonders about the "contradictory life of this great composer".[17] But there is no "contradiction". Wagner's spirituality can only be called spiritual evil, and for an evangelical Christian like Kavanaugh to even consider that there may have been genuinely Christian aspects to Wagner's "faith" is to fly in the face of all reason. Wagner was self-deluded, decadent, and quite possibly possessed.

The Classical Delusion

What is it that persuades Kavanaugh, and many others, to believe that there was some authentic Christianity in the life of someone like Wagner? It seems to be a classic case of the classical delusion: the idea that great art and beauty can only come from God, and that there is something spiritually ennobling, or even redeeming, in it. This is a blind spot in Christian thinking about art, and to understand its roots we have to go back to Paris in the year 1135.

The spiritual leader of the Abbey of St. Denis, Abbot Suger, was an inveterate art collector, and he sought to justify his love of art as being "to the glory of God". He did indeed find a philosophic basis for his work, which, according to the art historian Kenneth Clark, "has remained the basis of our belief in the value of art until today". But, Clark says, "it arose out of a typical medieval muddle. St. Denis, the patron saint of the Abbey, was confused with an Athenian monk named Denis, who was converted by St. Paul, and this Greek Denis was, quite wrongly, believed to be the author of a philosophical treatise called *The Heavenly Hierarchies*. Suger had this treatise translated from the Greek, and it was from this that he was able to give a theoretical justification of his love of beauty. He argued that we could only come to understand absolute beauty, which is God, through the effect of precious and beautiful things on our senses. He said 'The dull mind rises to truth through that which is material'."[18]

Here is a doctrine which says that God is beauty, and that we can only get to know God through beautiful things; so the more beautiful art, music or poetry is, the more closely it reflects God, and the more spiritual or godly it is in itself. It is this (false) identification of beauty with God which lies at the heart of the problem. This is what leads so many Christian music-lovers to think, "How could Wagner, or Mozart, or Tchaikovsky have created works of such beauty unless they were inspired by God? They must have been in touch with God somehow, despite their contradictory appearances. They must have been spiritual". Indeed, they were spiritual! Artistic creativity is not possible without some sort of spiritual inspiration. But to confuse spirituality and godliness is a dangerous error. Spiritualists and occultists, and the devil himself, are spiritual; indeed, the devil knows how to transform himself into an angel of light - and of captivating, radiant beauty. Satan can and does inspire beauty when it serves his ends.

It is a commonly held but utterly mistaken notion that the difference between godly and satanic things is clear-cut - godly things are beautiful, and satanic things are ugly, or "obviously" evil. This is simply not true. And as Christians we ought to know that the things that are great in man's eyes are not the things God has chosen; on the contrary, scripture actually declares that God has chosen the opposite things - the things we call foolish, uncultured, ignoble, weak and despised - to confound the great, glorious, wise, mighty and noble (see 1 Cor 1:26-29). But the church seems to be increasingly choosing according to man's wisdom - choosing the great, the talented and the powerful - and not only that, but adding what amounts to a blasphemous insult by claiming that man's way is God's way.

The cause of this blind spot is the idolising of music. When music becomes an idol, it blinds men to reason, and blinds Christians to spiritual reason. It is this obsessive love of music that leads Christians to desperately try to identify it with "spirituality", and we need to fight against idolatry and against anything that would bring us under the power of music. Indeed, (to return to Wagner), Christians need to seriously consider, not whether to go out and buy Patrick Kavanaugh's "recommended listening" records, but whether it can be spiritually healthy to be listening to the expression of a man with a depraved, deluded, anti-Christian mind. Wagner certainly knew how to express his spirit; but do we want to be on the receiving end of that spirit?

Stravinsky's reputation as the "enfant terrible" of early 20th century music is well founded. The uproar at the world première in Paris of his ballet *The Rite of Spring* in 1913 has become the stuff of legend. Subtitled "Scenes from Pagan Russia", it tells of pagan fertility rites in which a young virgin is chosen to dance to the death as a sacrifice, in order to ensure the return of Spring. At the première, "the audience demonstrated so vehemently that it was often impossible to hear the music". In the Second Part, "a cacophony of screaming and shouting filled the theatre ... the full extent of the disturbance which this historic score provoked may be realised from the fact that during the ensuing scuffle fifty people stripped themselves naked and, after being rounded up, landed in the Commissariat de Police ...".[19] "Never" said the music critic Roman Vlad, "had an audience heard music so brutal, savage, aggressive, and apparently chaotic; it hit the public like a hurricane, like some uncontrolled primeval force". But the power was attractive as well as disturbing. Several performances later, the Parisian critic Emile Vuillermoz wrote, "a secret power brings you back to every performance ... a kind of barbaric drunkenness seizes you ...". *The Rite of Spring* remains one of Stravinsky's most famous works, and is now acknowledged as a 20th century masterpiece. As we noted in Chapter 8, we eventually get used to new styles and new spirits, and what initially provoked outrage now raises only complacent smiles. But what forces were unleashed through this performance? Dare we, as Christians, ever "get used" to music like this?

Tippett is acknowledged to be Britain's greatest living composer. His music is dominated by New Age thought; one of his collections of essays is entitled "Moving Into Aquarius". His work is at the forefront of permissive thinking, like so many others in the arts; two of the main characters in his opera "The Knot Garden" (1966-70) are a homosexual couple. There is also an overtly spiritual dimension to his music. Talking about the inspiration for another of his operas, "The Midsummer Marriage", Tippett describes a spiritual vision he had of a stage scene: "a wooded hilltop with a temple, where a warm and soft young man was being rebuffed by a cold and hard young woman ... to such a degree that the collective magical archetypes take charge ... the girl ... rises through the stage to heaven ... the man ... descends through the stage floor to hell. But it was clear they would soon return. For I saw the girl later descending in a costume reminiscent of the goddess Athena, (who was born without father from Zeus's head) and the man ascending in one reminiscent of the god Dionysus, (who, son of earth-born Semele, had a second birth from Zeus's thigh)." Tippett recalls this unusual spiritual experience with awe: "Even as I write now the excitement of these first pictures comes back ... It is the feeling a creative artist has when he knows he has become the instrument of some collective imaginative experience - or, as Wagner put it, that a Myth is coming once more to life".[20] When one thinks of the sort of myths which Wagner brought to life, Tippett's excitement about the idea of a composer being a vehicle of some kind of spiritual, cosmic power has a chilling ring to it.

Britten, the leading light of British music until his death in 1976, led the way for moral revolution (as people in the arts world so often do) by openly declaring his homosexual relationship with the tenor Peter Pears, at a time when "coming out" and admitting homosexuality was a very rare and daring thing to do.

Stockhausen has spent the last twenty years at the forefront of avant garde music. He declares "The essential aspect of any music is always religious and spiritual".[21] But Stockhausen's religion and spirituality is Eastern. One of his pieces is called *Mantra*; another is called *Inori* (a Japanese word for prayer or meditation). Stockhausen has many New Age influences: his favourite reading is the Sufi mystic Hazrat Inayat Khan (see Chapter 19).

There is undoubtedly a spirituality about great composers. But only rarely is it a godly spirituality. Mostly it is simply an intuitive spiritual openness to whatever comes along. Because creating music is the prime aim and satisfaction of composers, they are not too worried from what source their creative urge comes. As we have seen, today, and right down through the ages, there have been some very dark and deceptive forces at work behind the inspiration of classical music, and the composers have been channels for those forces to work as they please.

Notes

1. C. S. Lewis, *The Great Divorce* (Fount Paperbacks, 1977) p. 74
2. Patrick Kavanaugh, *The Spiritual Lives of Great Composers* (Word UK, 1992) p. 79
3. *ibid.*, p. 63
4. *ibid.*, p. 69
5. *The Memoirs of Hector Berlioz*, trans. David Cairns (London: Gollancz) p. 462
6. Hector Berlioz, *Evenings with the Orchestra* (trans: Barzun, Chicago) p. 152
7. Kavanaugh, *op. cit.*, p. 88
8. *ibid.*, pp. 88, 89, 93
9. Alexandra Orlova, *Tchaikovsky, A Self-Portrait* (Oxford University Press, 1990) pp. 411-414
10. Kavanaugh, *op. cit.*, p. 99
11. Wilhelm Altmann (ed.), *Letters of Richard Wagner* (Dent and Sons, 1936) p. 102

12. Derek Watson, *Richard Wagner, A Biography* (J. M. Dent, 1979) p. 304
13. Watson, *op. cit.*, p. 304
14. Kavanaugh, *op. cit.*, p. 101
15. Watson, *op. cit.*, p. 304
16. *ibid.*, p. 316
17. Kavanaugh, *op. cit.*, pp. 102-103
18. Kenneth Clark, *Civilization* (BBC / John Murray, 1969) p. 30
19. Neil Tierney, *The Unknown Country, A Life of Igor Stravinsky* (Robert Hale, 1977), p. 61
20. Michael Tippett, *Moving Into Aquarius* (Paladin Books, 1974), pp. 54-55
21. Karlheinz Stockhausen, 3rd Seminar on *Stimmung*, 3rd August 1972

Chapter 11

Anatomy Of A Genius

The principal mark of genius is not perfection but originality, the opening of new frontiers.

Arthur Koestler

Nothing exemplifies "the classical delusion" more than people's attitudes to Mozart. Those who are not acquainted with classical music find Mozart's music dry and boring. Others, like the romantic composer Schumann, see it as light, graceful and innocuously charming. Still others (including many classical musicians today) worship Mozart almost as a god. Those who belong to the first category have not realised that classical music is an acquired taste. Once the taste is acquired, it usually becomes something of an addiction. By "addiction" I mean more than just enthusiastic devotion; I mean behaviour that has become compulsive (whether physically or psychologically), where the object of your devotion starts to control you, where you become to some extent dependent on it. In fact, there seems to be a link between acquired taste and addiction. Even at the level of physical addictions such as alcohol, the taste for the drink first has to be acquired. No-one likes whisky, or even beer, at the first taste. The same is usually true even of mildly addictive stimulants like coffee. (I am not dealing here with the question of whether addictive things, or acquired tastes, are "wrong". My point is that classical music is both an acquired taste and addictive, and that these two qualities are linked.)

In the case of music, it does indeed take some time to get onto the wavelength of Mozart's expressive language, or Bach's, or Bartók's. But once you have "tuned in", it is an experience that you want to return to, perhaps because it is outside of the normal "wavelengths", beyond the normal modes of experience. Whatever the case, the desire to return to the experience of classical music can soon grow into a full-blown addiction - a compulsive habit, a dependency that is very difficult to break. This sort of addiction is, however, quite permissible in society (which is why it is not usually called an addiction); in fact, the greater your addiction, the more cultured and respectable you are. The chief addicts of all are the musical geniuses, the great composers and performers; these people set the standards for culture by their art.

Mozart epitomises musical genius; he is often credited with the title of "the world's greatest composer". He was raised in the staunchly Catholic environment of 18th century Austria, and indeed frequently mentions God and spiritual matters in his letters. But like so many composers, his Christianity was a strange mixture of contradictory elements. Patrick Kavanaugh calls Mozart's faith "deeply personal. It bore the marks of Roman Catholicism, Protestant influence, 18th century Enlightenment thinking and the Freemason movement".[1]

Mozart And Freemasonry

Mozart was himself a Freemason and wrote several works for the Order, including a major opera (The Magic Flute), which is a Masonic allegory. "The consciousness of his membership in the order permeates his entire works. Not only The Magic Flute but many other of his works are Masonic, even though they reveal nothing of this quality to the uninitiated".[2]

Kavanaugh tries to play down the importance of Freemasonry in Mozart's life, quoting Mozart scholar Katherine Thomson: "it was not inconsistent for a Freemason to be a Christian".[3] But the quote is out of context; all it means is that there were plenty of Freemasons who claimed to be Christians (as there still are today). Elsewhere in her book, Thomson says: "Mozart's views were clearly unorthodox; his association with members of the Illuminati would be enough to condemn him in the eyes of the [Catholic] p*Anatomy Of A GeniusAnatomy Of A Genius*riests".[4] She also remarks, "It is clear that the Masonic ideals ... meant far more to him than the teachings of the Catholic Church".[5]

The Illuminati - Witchcraft and Politics

The Illuminati was a politically subversive organization founded in 1776 which soon found its way into the Freemason movement. It was banned in 1784 but has continued as a secret society to the present day. I first came across the name of the Illuminati in the testimony of a man named John Todd, who was converted to Christianity from witchcraft in the 1970's. He had been a high-ranking member of the Illuminati, and claimed that they are now a worldwide organization, led by the Rothschild family and including amongst their membership some of the most powerful financial/political leaders and organizations in the world, including the Rockefeller, Dupont, Kennedy and Onassis families, and the late Queen Juliana of the Netherlands. Todd even claimed that the occult-looking seal which appears at the left hand side of the reverse of the American one dollar bill is actually the seal of the Illuminati, and that its date *(MDCCLXXVI)* commemorating the beginning of a "New Order" refers not to *4th July* 1776 (the date of American Independence) but to *1st May* 1776 (the founding date of the Illuminati). The religion of the Illuminati is witchcraft, according to Todd; and he pointed out that the initiation rites he went through as a witch are identical to Masonic initiation rites.

The Grand Master of Mozart's lodge, Otto von Gemmingen, and the Master of the neighbouring lodge with whom they shared a temple, Ignaz von Born, were both Illuminati members; both were friends and patrons of Mozart. "Illuminati meetings were held by night at a lonely grotto at Aigen, near Salzburg ... attended by Count Gilowsky, one of the Illuminist leaders, 'with his friends von Amman, Mozart and Barisani'."[6] Masonic and humanist ideals pervade Mozart's music. "The humanist message can hardly be missed ... Masonic ideas and Masonic aims emerge, if one follows the music, in many of Mozart's best known symphonies and concertos - and their expression may, indeed, account for some of the undying appeal of these works".[7]

"A Subversive Artist"

Mozart's music has a definite message; his style has a definite spirit behind it. "Mozart hoped to change men's hearts through his music, to win them for an understanding of the ideas of the Enlightenment".[8] The message is subversive politically, morally and spiritually. *The Magic Flute* was "an arm of middle-class liberalism, a covert attack on the government, and a splendid work of propaganda for the Freemasons".[9]

The 3 Mozart operas which Patrick Kavanaugh recommends are *The Magic Flute,* which, apart from its political subversiveness, is full of Masonic (i.e. witchcraft) symbolism and philosophy (the opera ends with a hymn to the Egyptian gods Isis and Osiris); *The Marriage of Figaro,* which contains a fair deal of the bourgeois revolutionary propaganda current in the 1780's, just prior to the French Revolution; and *Don Giovanni,* the story of the sexual exploits of an aristocratic nobleman. *Don Giovanni* is morally subversive, and it inspired outrage for years after its first performance. Charles Rosen, perhaps the most perceptive modern critic of Mozart, calls it "an attack, both full frontal and oblique, upon aesthetic and moral values",[10] and he points out that Mozart knew exactly how to employ the sensuous qualities of music, music's appeal to the flesh, to add to the power of the story. Indeed, Mozart's choice of subject may only have been an excuse to indulge in his genius for exploiting the pure sensual power of music. Rosen draws attention to the fact that the philosopher Kierkegaard viewed *Don Giovanni* as "the only work that perfectly embodies the essentially erotic nature of music", and adds: "perhaps no other composer used the seductive physical power of music with the intensity and the range of Mozart. The flesh is corrupt and corrupting". Rosen discerns a "violence and sensuality at the centre of Mozart's work ... something shockingly voluptuous ... Mozart is a subversive artist."[11]

Mozart: A False Prophet?

Mozart's work attacked the established values and substituted new, alternative values. Haydn stands in contrast to Mozart: Haydn's music was generally a simple, straightforward expression of his own genial personality, some would say of his Christianity. Mozart, on the other hand, seemed to gain his inspiration from powers outside himself. His genius exploited all the powerful forces of music to create an uncompromising, radically subversive, dangerous art. Those who, like the 19th century composer Schumann, see nothing but lightness, grace and charm in Mozart's music, see only the surface appearance, something very akin to the "sweetness and light" appearance of the false prophet, the "wolf in sheep's clothing" described by Jesus. Are there any grounds for calling Mozart a false prophet? It certainly seems clear enough that, although he owned a nominal Christianity, Mozart actually attacked and subverted the values of genuine Christianity at every level.

Charles Rosen comments: "The sheer beauty, prettiness even, of so much of what he composed, masks the uncompromising character of his art. It cannot be fully appreciated without recalling the uneasiness and even dismay that it so often evoked in its time".[12]

The power of music was everything to Mozart. He exploited the power of sound in a way no-one had done before, and in this respect his music exhibits a belief in the power, even the spiritual power, of sound - an important concept in New Age thought, as we shall discover in Chapter 17. In *The Magic Flute,* Prince Tamino sings that the flute's

sound of magic has the power
to guard us safe in death's dread hour

This kind of language, typically Masonic, and essentially occult in its ideas, was a part of Mozart's ideology. What spiritual influences he opened himself up to we shall never know. As far as his Freemasonry was concerned, Mozart probably did not know himself; in common with most Freemasons, he would have been unaware of the identical nature of his initiation ceremony to that of witchcraft, and unaware of the spiritual forces to which he was thereby opening himself. But as Sir Michael Tippett's account of his own inspirational process (see Chapter 10) suggests, the crowning experience of artistic life, and one of the supreme expressions of genius, is when a composer, performer, poet or painter becomes a vehicle for "magical archetypes", "Myths", and "collective imaginative experiences", forces and powers greater than themselves. In fact, in *Moving Into Aquarius*, Tippett admiringly quotes Mozart's claim that he "received" his compositions into his mind whole and entire, "finished before it had begun". Referring to one of Mozart's letters, Tippett notes that "he said that his best works of music appeared to him all at once, as though the time taken to have sounded them were reduced to a single moment. Then all he did was write it down ..."[13]

Testing The Spirits

A genius is usually defined as someone with extraordinary instinctive, imaginative, creative or inventive power. But there is more to genius than this. The nature of genius is spiritual and inspirational. This is why Arthur Koestler remarked that "the principal mark of genius is originality, the opening of new frontiers". A genius is, primarily, a medium - a vessel or channel for "forces" to work through in an unprecedented way. As Christians, we recognize that these forces are spiritual. That Mozart's inspiration was spiritual cannot be doubted. The nature of that spirituality is another question; but to observe the three aspects of his life and work which we have briefly discussed here - his Masonic involvement, his exploitation of the sensual power of music, and the disturbingly subversive nature of his work - is to gain a perspective which suggests one answer to that question.

The recent trend of whole-hearted, uncritical acceptance by Christians of classical music as an entirely positive and godly thing is, to me, a cause for concern. In the past few years I have met many Christians who have told me they are "developing a taste for classical music" or "really getting into that classical stuff". They seem to be implying that this marks a new stage in their spiritual progress, that they are somehow more godly because of it. They don't realise they may as well be telling me that they're developing a taste for red wine or holidays in Switzerland. All they're doing is letting me know that they're getting more interested in the world. There's nothing wrong with Swiss holidays or wine, but nobody would call me more spiritually mature for drinking wine or going on holiday! But classical music is becoming subconsciously identified in many Christians' minds with godliness.

Classical music should not be identified with godliness; it should be identified as part of the world, its system, and its culture. Our whole view of music depends on our understanding of "the world" - a subject we will examine in detail in Chapter 12.

Notes

1. Kavanaugh, op. cit., p. 51
2. Alfred Einstein, Mozart (Cassell, 1946) p. 82
3. Kavanaugh, op. cit., p. 51
4. Katherine Thomson, The Masonic Thread in Mozart (Lawrence and Wishart, 1977) p. 172
5. ibid., p. 172
6. ibid., p. 17
7. ibid., back cover
8. ibid., p. 159
9. Charles Rosen, The Classical Style (Faber and Faber, 1972) p. 321
10. ibid., p. 324
11. ibid., p. 324-5
12. ibid., p. 325
13. Tippett, op. cit., p. 15

Part II

MUSIC, THE WORLD AND THE CHURCH

We are the music makers,
And we are the dreamers of dreams;
Wandering by lone sea-breakers,
And sitting by desolate streams;-
World-losers and world-forsakers,
On whom the pale moon gleams:
Yet we are the movers and shakers
Of the world for ever, it seems.

Arthur O'Shaughnessy, ***The Music Makers***

And oftentimes, to win us to our harm,
The instruments of darkness tell us truths
Win us with honest trifles, to betray us
In deepest consequence.

Shakespeare, ***Macbeth***

The only ultimate disaster that can befall us is to feel ourselves at home on this earth.

Malcolm Muggeridge

Chapter 12

The Origins Of Culture

If you know the past, you know the future.

Harry S. Truman

We have discussed some of the powers for which music can be a medium, and we have seen that music's power can be used and abused in the hands of both musicians and listeners. But *what is the real purpose of music*? If we can answer that, we will be able to see more clearly how the power should be used. Music always has a purpose. It is always a means to an end. What is that end? And why do we, as Christians, use music? This section is about music's purpose, and I want to look from a biblical perspective to examine, first of all, the origins of music.

Inspiration, Invention and Independence

We know there is music in heaven. The nature of that music, however, is unknown. We may suppose that it compares to earthly music as the resurrection body compares to the earthly body. It is another dimension entirely, far greater and more glorious. Heavenly music is of a different order. We only know earthly music, so we can only talk about that. But here the Bible can help us, because interestingly enough, it tells us about the origins of music on earth.

Adam was not given any musical instruments, apart from his voice. He was told to do things - namely, have a family, replenish and subdue the earth, and tend the garden (Gen 1:28, 2:15). That was his "creative outlet". There was, of course, no technology in Eden, and there is nothing in Scripture to indicate that God intended Adam to invent anything. Indeed, Adam and his descendants through Seth to Noah did not invent anything. Everything that is recorded of the line of Seth is to do with the fact that they had a relationship with God. In the days of Seth's son Enos, "men began to call on the name of the Lord"; Enoch "walked with God", until "God took him"; and Noah, "a just man and perfect in his generations ... walked with God" (Gen 4:26, 5:24, 6:9). Noah built the ark, of course, but that was not his invention; it was an act of obedience to God's specific command and design.

Cain's Seed And The Origins Of Culture

However, with Cain and his line, it is exactly the opposite. None of Cain's descendants are recorded as having any relationship with God. But they were extremely active in the field of invention, and they are of special interest to us because in their activities we find the origins of all the world's culture, including music.

Cain began it by building a city. Five generations later, Lamech had three sons: Jabal, "the father of all that dwell in tents and have cattle"; Jubal, "the father of all such as handle the harp and organ"; and Tubal-cain, "an instructor of every worker in brass and iron" (Gen 4:17-22). In their activities we see the beginnings of the world's cultural system. Cain built a city, thus initiating a *political* system. Jabal kept cattle - not for meat, for everyone was vegetarian before the flood, but to trade with - thus initiating *commerce and business*. Jubal was the first musician, and instigated the *arts*; and Tubal-cain was a metal-worker, a craftsman who could be seen as the father of *technology* and scientific knowledge as well as of industry.

All this begs an interesting question: why did all these things originate in the line of Cain? Where did their astonishing inspiration come from? I believe there is a clear answer. God gave Adam the garden to tend, and He wanted Adam to walk in close fellowship with Him. Seth's descendant Enoch did "walk with God", and Noah was "a preacher of righteousness". But Cain's descendants did not walk with God; in fact, they strove for the opposite - independence from God. Here lies the key to the inspiration behind all these first inventions - they represent the trend away from God, the desire to be independent from Him.[1]

To sum up, then, the Bible shows us two groups of people: the first group had relationship with God, strove for dependence on Him, and invented nothing; the second group had no relationship with God, strove for independence from Him, and invented or initiated many things.

Consider the benefits of inventions to mankind. What tremendous progress man has made in civilization and culture! And yet, at the same time, how far he has moved from God! It seems that the more the world "progresses", the more godless it becomes. It is a thought worthy of our serious consideration that scientific, artistic, economic and political progress (what we might call the progress of civilization) and spiritual progress are quite different things. Just because civilization is progressing does not mean that people are drawing closer to God; in fact, often it means exactly the opposite.

Inventions can certainly be said to have benefited man physically, but spiritually, are we any better off for all our inspirations, genius, and progress in knowledge? The answer is no, for the simple reason that these things can never bring us closer to God. They do not have to pull us away from God, but they can never bring us closer to Him. The progress of civilization brings no spiritual benefit to man.

Consider one single fact. The places in the world today where Christianity is the strongest, the purest, the most vibrant, and the most effective, are the places where persecution (by "civilized" people) deprives the Christians of most of the benefits of "civilization".

Indeed, in the second half of the 20th century, we are teetering on the brink of self-destruction as a result of our misuse of our own inventions, and the more pessimistic observers of our present world consider that if we do not destroy ourselves with atomic weapons, we are likely to do so by means of global pollution and ecological imbalance. Even if we consider only the physical benefits of inventions, we still find problems. The car, for example, has been responsible for the deaths of millions of people through accidents. A small price to pay for the benefits? I don't know whether we can say that. What price a man's soul?

I realize it is rather unconventional to question the moral basis for our whole civilization! We tend to take it for granted that civilization is a good, even a godly thing; and you may be asking: "What's wrong with business, politics, the arts, and science?" We need to be careful here. There's nothing wrong with the concept of politics in itself, that is, an organized system of government. Neither are cities wrong in themselves, or trade, or music. God has His own politics - the laws, ways and values of His kingdom. The fulfilment of all things is a city, New Jerusalem. These things aren't wrong in themselves. It's *the spirit behind their origins in this world* that's wrong, the spirit that led to their invention, which was *independence from God*. They are the product of an ungodly spirit. So this means that politics in this world is tainted, because it has a bad root. The same goes for all the elements of culture. In fact, everything of the earth, the whole creation, is destined to be burned up. Why? Because it's all tainted. The whole creation will one day be redeemed, and "corruption will put on incorruption". But only God can do this work of redemption (contrary to the thoughts of some musicians who believe that we can "redeem" music for God now). Until then, all the elements of civilization and culture have one factor in common: their root in independence from God. They continually maintain this independence; they can all keep on living and working quite happily independently of God.

Of course, there is a sense in which all things are continually upheld by God, and without Him everything would cease. But I am talking of the way people can carry on their life without acknowledging or relying on God for their inspiration, strength or success. They may even openly profess hatred for God. They know this will not disturb their success. The world has proved it. A city and its political system can run on its own steam. A business doesn't need God to help it along. Man can do it himself. Likewise the arts, science and technology - man can create and invent and do his own thing, without being dependent on God.

The Things That Are In The World

These foundations of civilization and culture are the basic constituents of what John calls "the world" (1 Jn 2:15). That term (*kosmos* in the original Greek) does not refer to the physical created earth (the Bible always calls this "the earth"; it is a different word in Greek). "The world" in the Bible always means a spiritual system, an ordered system with a mind and purpose behind it. The primary idea behind the word *kosmos* is that of orderly arrangement or adornment. (*Kosmos* is, in fact, once translated "adorning" in the Bible, in 1 Peter 3:3. Our English word "cosmetic" is derived from the same word.)

It is important to be very clear about this. In the New Testament, the word "world" is invariably used in a bad sense: "Be not conformed to this world"; "Love not the world ... for all that is in the world ... is not of the Father"; "the whole world lies in wickedness" (Rom 12:2; 1 Jn 2:15-

16, 5:19). This does not mean that ordered systems are bad things in themselves. God also has a system, His "world". That involves His laws, His politics, His ethics. One day His system will take over this earth: "The kingdoms of this world are become the kingdoms of our Lord and of His Christ" (Rev 11:15). But the world we now live in is a very different system indeed. Scripture clearly tells us that this world is the devil's system. The mind behind the system is that of its ruler, "the prince of this world", Satan. Scripture clearly distinguishes the earth from the world. "The earth is the Lord's, and everything in it" (Ps 24:1); It is His creation; but the world, according to scripture, is ruled by the devil, and everything in it has been given to him (Lk 4:5,6). The spirit of independence from God originates, of course, with Satan; he is the one who passed it on to Cain and his descendants. This is why the term "the world" is used in a bad sense in the gospels and epistles, and why all the elements of culture and civilization which make up our world system are tainted.

The Pinnacle Of Culture - Babylon

Eventually, the Bible tells us, this world system will culminate in the full-blown kingdom of antichrist. That is the way all these things are heading. At that time every element in the system will have become totally anti-christian. The flood, although it destroyed the seed of Cain, did not destroy the spirit of independence, neither did it destroy the devil; so the world system soon re-began its development. Within a few generations, Nimrod was building a kingdom and a tower to the heavens in Babel. Babel is the early name of Babylon, the great city and empire which ruled over all the known world in Nebuchadnezzar's day. But Babylon does not only belong to the past. It reappears again in Bible prophecy in the book of Revelation, concerning the age prior to the return of Christ. Here, "Babylon" signifies the world system at its anti-christian height, and at that point the world has become so ungodly that Christians are no longer instructed to be "in it but not of it": God calls His people to "come out of her" before He destroys the entire system (Rev 18:4).

It is instructive to note that the very same four foundational elements of culture found in Genesis 4 appear again in Revelation 18 - the description of Babylon and her destruction. *Politics* is there: Babylon is itself a city, and the political system has now evolved into a worldwide empire (or, to put it in more modern terms, a "one-world system"). The political rulers, "the kings of the earth", are described in Rev 18:3,9,10. *Commerce* is there: a large part of the chapter refers to merchants and their trade - the economic system by which Babylon existed (verses 3,11-19); then in verse 22 "harpers, musicians, pipers, trumpeters" are mentioned - emphasizing music particularly among the *arts*; and finally "craftsmen", representing perhaps some of the visual arts (sculpture, architecture) as well as *technology* and industry. The four major elements of the world system, politics, commerce, the arts, and technology, are present at the end of the world; and their fulfilment is seen to be totally anti-God and anti-christian: "In her (Babylon) was found the blood of prophets, and of saints, and of all that were slain upon the earth" (Rev 18:24). Rebellious pride and independence from God is at the root of it all. That's the world.

Notes

1. The phrase 'the trend away from God' is borrowed from Watchman Nee. In *Love Not The World* (Kingsway) he examines the origin and meaning of the world, and his book pis recommended as helpful further reading on the subject.

Chapter 13

Touching The Devil's System

The older the world grows, the more heated becomes the conflict between Christ and Antichrist.
Dietrich Bonhoeffer

The Church and the world are opposites, in the sense that the world carries on independent of God, not acknowledging Him or desiring Him; whereas the Church, on the other hand, is dependent upon God for its life every second, just as the children of Israel needed fresh manna every day. Jesus says, "Without me you can do nothing". Paul says, "We are not sufficient in ourselves". So it is, always, for the Christian. As soon as the life and activity of God stops, the Church dies. What is of *God* is entirely dependent on God. But everything in the *world* carries on as if it had a life of its own, independently of God, as part of the trend away from God.

It is important to understand this correctly. I am not identifying the world with physical things, and the Church with spiritual things. Still less am I suggesting that physical things are bad and spiritual things are good. That is a heresy which has surfaced in Christendom from time to time, but it is utterly unbiblical. On the contrary, the truth is that on the one hand, spiritual things are not necessarily good or godly, but can be evil; and on the other hand, as Christians we are called to work with physical things every day, and there is nothing inherently evil about anything physical. This is why I stressed in Chapter 2 that physical sounds or musical notes cannot be evil in themselves.

In the same way we have to remember that when we talk about "the world" (in the sense that the Bible uses the term), we are not talking about a physical entity. The Bible always calls the planet we live on, and the physical environment we inhabit, "the earth". When we talk about the world, the *kosmos*, we are not talking about anything physical, but about a spiritual system which is rooted in the spirit of independence from God, masterminded by "the prince of this world", the devil, and which will culminate in the kingdom of the antichrist. This is why the Bible can talk about the world as being evil, without implying that physical things are evil. We are called to live in the midst of this ungodly system, much as Daniel was called to live in Nebuchadnezzar's Babylon, but we are also called to be "not of it". That means *we are never to participate in the world's spirit and purpose*. Daniel never once compromised with Babylon (though for him it meant facing death in the lion's den). Likewise, we are never to identify with the world's spirit of independence from God, even though we may be doing many things in business, or the arts, or science, which were originally inspired and designed with that independence in mind.

This, of course, is not an easy job! That's why Paul tells us that "those who use this world should act as not abusing it, for the fashion of this world is passing away" (1 Cor 7:31). So whenever we touch the world's system - and we all do to some extent - we must tread carefully, knowing we are touching something which is in essence anti-God, regardless of how harmless it may seem. We have to be wise. There is a great danger to the Church here; we can so easily be convinced that the things of the world are harmless, even beneficial, although God says the opposite. Money is a good example. We all need to use money, and we can use it for God's work or to feed the poor, but the Bible still calls it "filthy lucre", recognising that money is not by any means harmless. A Christian friend of mine once objected to this thought, saying "Doesn't the Bible tell us to 'befriend mammon'?" His objection was actually a good case in point! For Jesus does not tell us to "befriend mammon" at all; he tells us to "make friends to ourselves by means of unrighteous mammon", which is a different matter altogether; and as if to emphasize the fact that money is not neutral or harmless, Jesus goes out of his way to not call it "money" but instead gives it the decidedly derogatory name of "unrighteous mammon" (Lk 16:11).

Gullibility - The Christian's Great Danger

Jesus also made the point that Christians are prone to be gullible. He remarked that "the children of this world are wiser in their generation than the children of light" (Lk 16:8). We recognise evil and ungodliness easily enough when it is blatantly evil and ungodly (but then, so does the world, for the most part. The daily newspapers are just as outraged and shocked by crime, vice and scandal as Christians are. Outright evil is obvious to everybody). However, we are notoriously bad at recognising evil when it looks innocent and innocuous. In fact, we tend to defend harmless looking things on the extraordinarily unscriptural principle that they are more likely to be godly if they appear harmless - as if we were completely unaware that the devil is a deceiver by nature who "masquerades as an angel of light". The prevalence of this attitude is quite astonishing. Perhaps it derives in part from a misunderstanding of what is meant by "worldliness".

The Disappearance Of "Worldliness"

Christians of an earlier generation tended to identify "worldly" things with "sinful" things ("dance halls and jewellery are worldly" meant "dance halls and jewellery are sinful"). This gave rise to a legalism which was unable to justify itself, because nowhere in scripture does it say that those things are sinful. But scripture does often say that certain behaviour is "worldly" or "of the world". However, the biblical definition of "the world" was often not properly understood or explained. So, in the past few decades, in a backlash against that legalism, the baby has been thrown out with the bath-water, and the word "worldly" now means nothing at all to most Christians, except a laughable term used by old-fashioned Christian prudes and legalists.

The business, politics, arts and science that go on in this world are not in themselves sinful or inherently evil, but they are "worldly" by definition, simply because they're part of the world's system. However, the current Christian viewpoint on involvement with the world seems to be "if it's not sinful, there can't be anything wrong in it; go ahead and do it, get involved." And because there isn't anything inherently sinful in music, business, etc., Christians feel quite free to behave like anyone else, as long as they don't break God's commandments. But this is a dangerous misunderstanding of scripture. Touch the world, and you touch a minefield of anti-God sentiment, a purpose designed to build the kingdom of the prince of this world, a system devised by him and under his dominion, whose principle is independence from God. Don't be deceived! I always have reservations when I hear people say "music is a gift from God - of course you should use it, you should stay in it for God". My reservations are not because I think that there is anything wrong with living and working "in the world"; we are commanded to do that. Neither is it because I think that music is wrong or sinful. Rather, I fear that these people are failing to discern between the Christian use of music, and music as part of the world's system. And I think that this distinction needs to be made clear.

Getting Into The World for God

I am even more disturbed when I hear people say that we should "get into music (or sport, or business, or politics) for God". I see that as a contradiction in terms, because I think it's a practical impossibility.

I was a musician before I was a Christian. In seeking to become a good musician, I made music my god. I devoted myself to it. I gave it my time, my money, my energy. I was selfishly ambitious, egotistical, ruthless, single-mindedly obsessed with music. That's the only way to get anywhere in the world. That's how I got as far as I did in the profession, and the same goes for everyone I've ever met who has "made it" in music. They love music more than anything else. They have to. They'd never make it otherwise.

Chetham's School of Music in Manchester (where I worked for some years) thoroughly grills its young hopefuls at their auditions to ensure that music is the all-consuming passion of their lives. I understand that - it has to be that way. The same goes for sport, or anything else you want to succeed in. You can't have any other goals besides the one you're pursuing, because *other goals are other gods.*

Of course, it frequently happens that God saves successful businessmen, and musicians, and politicians, and continues to use them where they are in the world. And I can tell you (from personal experience as well as from the testimonies of many such men and women) that God has to do a lot of breaking of powers in these people's lives. Not only must outright sins be dealt with, but also that independent spirit in which they pursued success, the spirit of the world, all their ambition, pride and ego, must be broken and laid at the foot of the cross; it must be thoroughly dealt with and rooted out, and it must never be taken up again. When you meet a Christian who has been through this "mill", you can tell the difference it has made to them. Sadly, many compromise along the way, and like the children of Israel in the promised land, only half deal with their enemies; the result is that they end up as half-hearted Christians, compromised and trapped by the system.

The Dilemma Of Compromise

However, the situation where God saves someone who has already become successful in this world is a different matter from Christians who want to "get into" an area of the system "for God". My problem with such people is that I cannot conceive how they are going to be able to do it with any degree of success, without recourse to ego, ambition, independence, ruthlessness and the rest of the attitudes which, though some of them may be neutral in themselves, contribute to the spirit of the world when they are used for things other than God. Such people are either going to try to be good Christians (in which case they will lack the necessary drive, because they'll refuse to be ruthlessly single-minded or obsessively ambitious for anything except God, and so they'll lack the qualities to push their way to the top; or else they'll go the other way - compromise with God, throw themselves into their career and get carried away on the world's principles, professing Christianity all the while, but in reality having left far behind the principles of God. I just don't see how it's possible to reconcile the two. Paul had very good reason to instruct his converts to remain as they were when they got saved - not to seek to be something different "for God" (1 Cor 7:17-24). God chooses people in a certain calling for a specific reason. Today we seem to have forgotten this principle.

Dependence

Wherever you are called, and whatever you do, the important thing is that you "do all to the glory of God" (1 Cor.

10:31). That means that God gets the glory, not you. This can only happen when we have laid down our own strengths, ego, desire and ambition, when we have come to a point of realising that we are "not sufficient in ourselves" (2 Cor 3:5).

Once this truth dawns upon us in reality, we are on the right path - God's way, which is always the exact opposite to the way of the world. We need to be constantly conscious of our helplessness. If I get excited about a project, trust in my natural ability, and start to get self-confident, I am in danger, because I'm losing sight of my own helplessness and insufficiency. On the other hand, if I am not excited or inspired and have no self-confidence, I need God's help for a different reason - because I am aware of my insufficiency; and knowledge of our own insufficiency and our dependence on God is what the Christian life is all about.

Understanding The Purpose

We can now go on to look in more detail at some of the ways in which the world's ideas about the purpose of music have worked their way into the Church. We need to clearly understand the roots and principles at work in these various ideas, and to ask whether we as Christians can really have an alternative purpose in music to that of the world. It is vital for us to know these things. They are not abstract theories and principles, but practical guidelines for life.

Chapter 14

Witchcraft In The Church - The Abuse of Manipulative Power

Where God built a church, there the devil would also build a chapel.

Martin Luther

It is now time to look again at some of the "powers" discussed in earlier chapters, and examine them in more detail so that we can see how they are being applied in music today, both in the world and in the Church.

I want first to take a closer look at the problems associated with manipulative power, particularly in relation to "praise and worship" music in church. Although I am talking here mainly to musicians, it is equally important that congregations appreciate the principles involved. If you are a member of a congregation, you are on the receiving end of all this music, and you too need to understand how musicians - for better or worse - can lead and control their audiences.

Does The Congregation Know ... ?

If you are a musician you are probably aware of the power in your hands to control an audience or congregation. Let's presume that you understand about using the principles of harmony, key change, rhythm and volume to make the congregation respond in a certain way. You will realise that with skill and experience you can get the congregation on their feet, singing, clapping, even dancing, simply by the use of these musical techniques. So you know that in this case it's not the influence of God's Spirit which has made that happen; it's the music. But does the congregation know that? The fact is, they are very probably quite unaware of it, and, sensing a power lifting their emotions and inspiring them to sing and clap, they presume it is God's Spirit. The same goes for quieter worship music. The sounds that you can produce entirely at will can create some very sweet, calm atmospheres which are deceptively similar to the peace and tranquillity of spirit that God's anointing can bring.

This confusion between God's anointing and what might be called "the anointing of the music" is becoming more and more common, as musical instruments, particularly keyboard technology, improve and become more widely available and acceptable in church worship. If Christian musicians are drawing on purely musical skills and techniques to produce desired effects, then they may be, albeit unwittingly, guilty of deceptive manipulation. In cases of spiritual deception, the deceivers are often deceived themselves. These are strong words, but music is a powerful medium, and if we end up presenting musical techniques to people and confusing those techniques with God's Spirit or anointing, then that is doubly dangerous. We cannot allow ourselves to be manipulators, or manipulated, in this way. The basic principle of witchcraft is the abuse of manipulative power - illicit control over other people's feelings, circumstances, thoughts and lives. That is not Christianity, and the principles of witchcraft have no place in the Church! It may well be that we are presently only seeing a small amount of abuse born of ignorance, but it could easily be the thin end of the wedge. Now is the time to take a radical stand against such attitudes.

It is certainly questionable whether congregations do understand what is happening in these worship times. Are they aware of the purely natural but powerful results obtainable from the clever use of good musical instruments, and do they recognise it for what it is, or do they confuse this with the presence of God? My fear is that the confusion is growing. Churchgoers are suddenly being exposed to high quality live music, and no-one is telling them the implications and the consequences of that. They don't really understand as they should what is going on, and some explanation from those "insiders" who do understand the techniques and principles involved is long overdue.

The End Of The Road?

Perhaps I am being over-dramatic, but I am increasingly concerned about what lies at the end of this road. Is it possible that, if Christians begin to lose the distinction between the genuine anointing of God and what we might call "the anointing of the music", they could be deceived into thinking that their meetings are richly anointed by God's presence, when in reality what they are getting is a subtle substitute - an emotionally satisfying "lift" or "relaxation", the psychological effects of which may be beneficial, but which has nothing to do with God's anointing, any more than the effects you might get from a work-out at the gym or a good movie? If this happens, there is great danger. The true presence of God might be entirely absent from that church's worship, but all the while they can remain convinced that the anointing is getting stronger at every meeting - because the musicians are getting better at every meeting.

(On a related subject, we must also beware of the idea that healings, miracles or other supernatural gifts and signs constitute an infallible proof of God's presence or approval. Psychologists use music in therapy, and psychosomatic symptoms can be "miraculously" relieved, given the right psychological conditions. The spiritualists also know all about healing and spiritual gifts, including prophecy; and in New Age circles music is especially cultivated for its healing qualities, and that includes physical healing. Spiritual powers from suspect sources, using music as a medium, may yet yield more apparently "miraculous" fruit. But let us be careful to discern, and not presume that where the effects are either beneficial or supernatural, or both, that it is God's power at work.)

A little spiritual learning is a dangerous thing, and "counterfeit anointings" ride on the back of unclear thinking, misunderstandings and half-formed theologies. Mistaking the power of music for the presence of God opens the door to all sorts of spiritual problems, because it gives us a false confidence that God is behind whatever we are doing. It is doubly easy for the devil to slip in a little error here, a little compromise there, and all the while the "anointing" appears to remain; "God is still with us". But in reality "the glory has departed", and a deception has been substituted.

The false prophets and teachers are waiting in the wings, ready to ride on the wave of "anointing" which credulous Christians take to be the indisputable sign of God's presence. Music certainly has links with genuine prophecy, as when Elisha called for a musician: "And it came to pass, when the minstrel played, that the hand of the Lord came upon him, and he said 'Thus saith the Lord...' " (2 Kings 3:15,16). But the same is true of false prophecy, and it is not difficult to make a link between the evocative power of music and the false prophets in Israel who prophesied "out of the imagination of their hearts" (Jer 23:16; Ezk 13:17). It is worth considering the nature of this false prophecy. I do not believe that the false prophets in Israel were malicious or evil people, deliberately trying to deceive the people and rule by the power of their words. I don't imagine for a minute that they were concocting "prophecies" from their own minds, knowing full well that they were doing so. I am convinced that they were deceiving themselves as well as others. I'm sure that they genuinely felt that they had "the mind of the Lord", that they were hearing from God. What gave them the basis for believing this? Was it a sense of a "presence", or an "anointing" that came upon them? Or was it the general approval of God's people that convinced them they were right? Or a confidence in their own righteousness and godliness? Or their position in the "church"? Any of these "signs" can convince someone enough to be confident that they are a true prophet. Could it happen today? Of course! Does it happen today? Of course! It could easily happen with Christian "minstrels" and those who come under their influence; and in Chapter 15 we shall look at one situation where it does seem to have happened.

Needed: Discernment

My own experience as a Christian musician playing in worship groups has taught me that musicians need to exercise careful discernment. Our role is to create a background and foundation for God's people to express themselves to Him in song. If the background we create helps them to do that, then it is a good thing, a proper and appropriate use of music. We also have to learn to recognise the times when God does move during times of worship in song; we have to learn to discern between the input of human spirits and the moving of God's Spirit, and we have to learn to respond appropriately. When God's presence comes, people sometimes want to sing stronger; sometimes they want to sing very quietly; sometimes they don't want to sing at all. The musicians must be on the front line of awareness, listening to God, the congregation and each other. There is certainly no room for being wrapped up in what you are playing.

The danger of confusion between God's Spirit and the power of the music is compounded by a growing fascination with the spiritual aspects of music in non-christian circles. I quoted in Chapter 2 the sound module advert which majored on phrases like "trance-like meditational rituals" and "mystical communion among players". The inference to be drawn from this sort of talk is that the new musical technology puts at your disposal all the ingredients for a spiritual experience. "As borders dissolve, traditions are shared" says the advert; and musical traditions are increasingly recognized as being closely linked to spiritual traditions.

This renewed interest in the spiritual effects of music is nowhere more apparent than in the "alternative spirituality" of the New Age, which has even produced its very own style. We will shortly examine in detail some of the principles behind New Age music; suffice to say at this point that in New Age circles, music is seen as a powerful catalyst, an agent of change, able like a drug to induce changes in consciousness ("altered states"). In psychological terms, it is seen as an important influence for changing thought and behaviour (like hypnosis); in religious terms, it is a medium through which to "invoke" a higher power or presence (like meditation or spiritualist seances).

Spiritual Sounds

In our earlier discussion of the physical aspects and effects of music, I made it clear that there is no inherent moral characteristic, either good or evil, in any sound, no matter where it originated. But we are now considering the *use* of sound, and it is worthwhile asking: if we do want to use these "spiritual" sounds of which the advert speaks so compellingly, *why* do we want to use them? What is it about the sound that appeals to us? We do have to be careful that in our "conscience-free" borrowing of other sounds from other cultures, we are not subconsciously being drawn into the spiritual aesthetics of those cultures and alternative spiritualities. "Spiritual sounds" could easily become the 20th century equivalent of magnificent cathedrals, religious icons and incense - the aesthetic paraphernalia which creep in to Christianity and, eventually, become a substitute for God. I know many people who love going to church, not because they have any relationship with God, but because they love the "spiritual", "mystical" effects of the surroundings; the glorious architecture, the noble words, the chanting of monks, the fragrance of incense, the quiet and peace. Whatever that is, call it "religion" or whatever you like, it's not Christianity. But it's what most people in the world call "spiritual", and we need to be alert to the dangers inherent in such terminology. I may be repeating myself, but it cannot be stressed enough: "spiritual" is not synonymous with "godly" or "Christian".

Chapter 15

Music In The Last Days

> *"To you it is commanded, O people, nations, and languages, that at what time ye hear the sound of the cornet, flute, harp, sackbut, psaltery, dulcimer, and all kinds of musick, ye fall down and worship the golden image that Nebuchadnezzar the King hath set up: and whoso falleth not down and worshippeth shall the same hour be cast into the midst of a burning fiery furnace."*
>
> **Dan 3:4-6**

The role of music in the end times seems to be particularly important - and particularly suspect. The 3rd chapter of the book of Daniel is a historical account of King Nebuchadnezzar's command to worship a "golden image"; but it also seems to have an important prophetic significance for the last days. The king's decree was that whenever the people heard the sound of "all kinds of music", they must "fall down and worship the golden image" (Dan 3:5). Whoever refused would be thrown into a blazing furnace. The music was the cue to worship. But Nebuchadnezzar, the King of Babylon, is a type of the antichrist. *This music is the worship of antichrist.* Put that into the 20th century context and several possible scenarios become apparent.

The book of Revelation tells us that as the world reaches its culmination in the kingdom of antichrist, "the false prophet"[1] will command the people of the world to make an image of the beast (antichrist) and worship that image. If they refuse, they will forfeit their lives (Rev 13:14,15). There is clearly a parallel with what happened in Daniel's day.

Then, it was only a localised incident. But this is the worldwide fulfillment.

In the age of the music explosion, people in the world already do homage to "the great god music", and idolize its greatest exponents. Music has already become to them a religious thing, a matter of worship. As Christians, we realise that in worshipping music or its performers, these people are actually worshipping the mind behind the music - "the god of this world", who will eventually be manifested in the person of antichrist. Music is thus becoming a subconscious cue to worship. People may be ignorant of what or who they are really worshipping, but it is actually the spirit of antichrist.

It may happen that people will literally be called, at the sound of music, to fall down and worship antichrist or his image. The world will willingly do so; it will seem a wonderful thing to them. The god of this world, after all, must appeal to the world, because they all share that spirit, just as Christians all worship the true God, who "appeals to us" because He has given us His Spirit (see 1 Cor 2:12). It is disturbing to consider that if we, as Christians, become deceived into following the world's trends, we could become involved in the worship of antichrist. We certainly need to be aware of the danger. The devil is a deceiver, and his way is always to get people to do things without them realising they're doing it; and the world and its trends have a strong subconscious pull - even on Christians.

The above mentioned scenarios may seem serious enough. But I have to put forward a third possibility, more shocking and unbelievable by far. Is it possible, is it even credible, that Christians could be singing songs about Jesus Christ, believing that they are worshipping Him, and yet actually worshipping antichrist? It sounds too far-fetched to be true. But recent trends in the Church suggest that it could well be true, and that the danger is far more imminent, and the process far more advanced, than we might think.

The Rise Of The Prophet Musician

Lately a new type of leader has appeared on the Christian music scene - the "prophet musician". This phenomenon has arisen from an identification made between music and prophecy, based on the Old Testament accounts of "companies of the prophets" who had musical instruments with them (1 Sam 10:5), and Elisha's words "Now bring me a minstrel" when he wanted to prophesy (2 Kings 3:15). In recent years, musicians have in some charismatic churches been encouraged to "prophesy on their instruments", whether it be a flute or a drum kit. Now the trend has developed further, and the "prophet musician" is emerging as an important inspirational force in Christian music and worship.

One such man is Stephen Bennett, an Australian musician. He took part in "Cross Rhythms '95", a Christian Contemporary Music festival held in England, and brought a significant prophetic word to the festival. The prophecy said that God would "pour out His melodies from heaven", and promised fame, success and financial blessing to Christian musicians for the future. There was an exhortation to "redeem the sounds of the earth for the purposes of the Lord", reminiscent of the ideas found in LaMar Boschman's book *The Rebirth of Music* (see Chapter 19). But the most significant part of the prophecy was this: "... And as it is written in the book of Daniel, when you hear the sounds of all sorts of instruments and all styles of music, multitudes shall bow down and worship Jesus Christ as Lord of Lords and then, everybody dances in the street ..."[2]

I was astonished when I read this prophecy. Here was a man ostensibly using Daniel's prophecy of the worship of antichrist and reversing its meaning to make it refer to the worship of God. But nowhere in scripture is there any indication that anything of this sort will happen with the worship of God. On the contrary, there is every indication, as we have seen, that it will happen with the worship of antichrist. If Stephen Bennett's paraphrase of Daniel was simply an idea out of his own head, it would just be a case of very bad exegesis. But it is more than that - it is prophecy. I believe that he was indeed prophesying, but prophesying something completely different from what he thought. He was actually prophesying that the (original) words of Daniel will come true in the last days, and in the antichristian way that Daniel foretold - but that their fulfillment will involve Christians being deceived into believing that the antichrist is Jesus Christ, the Lord of Lords, and that Christian musicians will play an unwitting part in this deception. As they seek to "redeem the sounds of the earth" by assimilating into their music different world styles, and as they become increasingly prosperous, famous, and acceptable in the world, they will play into the cunning hands of the devil, become increasingly filled with the spirit of the world, and end up totally deceived by the counterfeit Christ, actually singing praise in the name of Jesus Christ, worshipping antichrist as the Lord of Lords, celebrating and "dancing in the street".

How The Impossible Can Happen

You are probably thinking to yourself, "Surely this is impossible! Such a terrible deception could never overtake Christians!" Such a reaction is understandable. But this is not the place for our own preconceptions and theories. We need to go to the Bible. This shocking scenario could only happen if the Bible tells us it could happen. It could only be possible:

a) if scripture indicates that the antichrist is a deceiver who plans to come as a "counterfeit Christ", as similar as possible to the real Christ, in order to deceive Christians and non-Christians alike.

b) if scripture indicates that it is possible for Christians to be deceived by a counterfeit Christ.

c) if scripture indicates that there will be a great falling away of Christians from the true faith before Jesus comes.

d) if the devil, the god of this world, had already been building up a subtle counterfeit over many years, gradually and imperceptibly corrupting the Church's worship so that it deviated little by little from worship of the true God to worship of a false god. This would necessarily involve a gradual change in allegiances, values, principles, lifestyle, theology, doctrines, and all the things that "worship" and "faith" incorporate. Finally, there would have to be examples of this kind of "turnaround" in scripture.

Let's examine these issues one by one

a) The nature of the antichrist:

Scholars of New Testament Greek tell us that the word *antichristos* "can mean either against Christ or instead of Christ, or perhaps combining the two, 'one who, assuming the guise of Christ, opposes Christ' (Westcott)".[3] Antichrist will only "assume the guise of Christ" because he wants to deceive Christians; and if the devil knows how to transform himself into an angel of light, antichrist will doubtless make a thorough job of transforming himself into the convincing appearance of Christ. 2 Thessalonians 2:4 confirms that the antichrist will "exalt himself above all that is called God, or that is worshipped; so that he as God sitteth in the temple of God, shewing himself that he is God."

b) The possibility of deception:

"There shall arise false Christs, and false prophets, and shall shew great signs and wonders; insomuch that, if possible, they shall deceive the very elect" (Mt 24:24). Jesus would not warn us of these things if there was no danger and no possibility of us being deceived. Twice in Matthew 24 He warns of false Christs and false prophets, and twice He tells His disciples not to believe rumours of Christ's arrival (Mt 24:23,26). In Luke's gospel He says, "Go not after them, nor follow them" (Lk 17:23).

Jesus also says, "Then shall they deliver you up to be afflicted, and shall kill you: and ye shall be hated of all nations for my name's sake. And then shall many be offended, and shall betray one another, and shall hate one another. And many false prophets shall arise, and deceive many." (Mt 24:9-11). This is clearly addressed to Christians, and concerns them, not the world. It is the Christians who are afflicted, killed and hated; it is likewise the Christians who then become "offended" and, out of fear, betray one another. (Such things have already happened many times under Communist persecution.) In the same way, it is the Christians who the false prophets come to deceive, just as antichrist assumes the guise of Christ because he wants to deceive Christians.

c) The falling away:

"That day [of Christ's coming] shall not come, except there come a falling away first, and that man of sin be revealed" (2 Thess 2:3). W.E. Vine says "The falling away signifies apostasy from the faith."[4] This apostasy is linked in the following verse to the arising of the antichrist as a counterfeit God (2 Thess 2:4, quoted above). It seems, in context, that the "falling away" is a falling away of Christians from the true God to the antichrist.

d) The formation of the counterfeit:

Many of the arguments in this book suggest that the devil has been working for a very long time to corrupt Christian worship and create counterfeits, and that there is plenty of evidence to show that Christians' values, principles, lifestyles and even doctrines are changing rapidly, and not for the better. Scripture and church history both show examples of a "turnaround" where people actually end up doing the opposite of what they think they are doing. Here are some scriptural examples:

(i) The Golden Calf.

When Aaron instructed the Israelites to break off their ear-rings, melted down the gold and made an image of a calf, he was not presenting the calf as an idol, a new or different god. He was presenting it as the image of the true God of Israel who delivered them from Egypt. When they saw it, they said, "These be thy gods, O Israel, which brought thee out of the land of Egypt." Aaron then declared a "feast to the Lord" for the following day, and they "offered burnt offerings, and brought peace offerings". They thought they were worshipping the God of Israel. But they were actually worshipping an idol, a false God. Without realising it, they had "corrupted themselves" - so much so that God wanted to destroy them, His own people, on the spot, and only Moses' intercession saved them. (See Ex 32:1-14)

(ii) The Pharisees.

The Pharisees were religious men who sincerely believed they were following God, and indeed prided themselves on their meticulous obedience to the law. They worshipped, they prayed daily, they fasted, they gave their time and money; they really believed they had a relationship with the living God. Yet Jesus told them bluntly that they were serving another god - the devil (Jn 8:44).

(iii) Peter's Warning.

The apostle Peter warns Christians that there will be false prophets among them who will bring in heresies "... and many shall follow their pernicious ways" (2 Pet 2:2). He urges them to "beware lest ye also, being led away with the error of the wicked, fall from your own stedfastness" (2 Pet 3:17). The insidious thing about false prophets is that they always claim to speak in the name of the true God, the God that you know. That is why they are so dangerous to Christians. They are counterfeits of the true prophets and true teachers, and their primary purpose is to corrupt and deceive, not the world, but the children of God.

(iv) Jesus' Warning.

Jesus also warned of false prophets in the Sermon on the Mount (Mt 7:15-20), and in the verses immediately following, He described a situation not dissimilar to the one we have been considering. "Not every one that saith unto me, Lord, Lord, shall enter into the kingdom of heaven; but he that doeth the will of my Father which is in heaven. Many will say to me in that day, Lord, Lord, have we not prophesied in thy name? and in thy name have cast out devils? and in thy name done many wonderful works? And then I will profess unto them, I never knew you: depart from me, ye that work iniquity" (Mt 7:21-23).

The scene Jesus describes is every bit as shocking as the one we are considering. Here are people who clearly believe themselves to be Christians, and who even have remarkable supernatural evidence to support their beliefs - and yet Jesus tells them they are "workers of iniquity". They are, not surprisingly, absolutely shocked to discover the truth. Even then, they call Him "Lord" and plead their case, as if hoping against hope that He might have mistaken their identity. But it is they who have made the mistake, and been terribly deceived. The lesson is as clear as it is unbelievable: you can name the name of Christ, worship Him, pray to Him every day, serve Him, have a "ministry", do supernatural signs and wonders in His name, and still be totally deceived, still be serving the wrong god, still be a "worker of iniquity", to whom Jesus will say "Depart from me".

Church history is littered with examples of Christian ministers within the mainstream Church who became deceived and ended up as leaders of false cults, claiming to serve Jesus Christ, but in reality lost in a mist of wrong doctrines and wrong motives. These are false prophets, whose teachings still lead thousands of ignorant Christians astray. The false prophets we need to beware of today are, of course, not the cult leaders, but the ones who are now within the mainstream Church. They are the "wolves in sheep's clothing" of which Jesus spoke, the dangerous deceivers who seem the most like genuine Christians.

Unwitting Vessels

In the book of Revelation, the false prophet commanded the people to worship antichrist. That is the final aim of all false prophecy. I say advisedly "the aim of all false prophecy" rather than "the aim of all false prophets". The false prophets, as we noted in Chapter 14, are usually deceived themselves. They have wrong motives in their hearts, to be sure. They are vessels for "seducing spirits"[5], speaking forth "doctrines of demons" (1 Tim 4:1). But they are unwitting vessels. They would be the last ones to think that they were leading people into the worship of antichrist. Yet we have seen a case in point; a sincere and talented worship leader bringing a dangerous and deceptive false prophecy. If my feeling is right, there will be more "prophet musicians" bringing many more "words" on similar lines.

A final thought for consideration. In Daniel's day, there were many thousands of Jews in captivity in Babylon. Yet we read of only three people who refused to worship Nebuchadnezzar's golden image. Were the rest all deceived? And if that situation is prophetic of antichrist's coming kingdom, what will be the percentage of deceived Christians in antichrist's kingdom? And how many will be led into that deception through "Christian music"?

Notes

1. In Rev 13:11 he is only referred to as "another beast", but in Rev 19:20 this beast is called "the false prophet".
2. *Cross Rhythms* magazine, Oct/Nov 1995
3. W.E. Vine, *Expository Dictionary of New Testament Words* (Zondervan, 1952), p. 61
4. *ibid.*, p. 73
5. Literally, "misleading spirits". The word in the original comes from a verb meaning "to cause to wander or lead astray".

Chapter 16

Magic In The Church - The Power of Impression

We can become drunk on music - there is no question about that. Music can have the effect of creating an emotional state in which the mind is no longer functioning as it should be, and no longer discriminating. I have known people to sing themselves into a state of intoxication without realizing what they were doing.

Martyn Lloyd-Jones

Manipulation and impression are closely related. We discussed impression in broad terms in Chapter 5, and now I want to speak particularly to "listeners" rather than performers. I have defined impression as the opposite of expression. *Expression* means giving voice (through words or music) to something that is a part of you, already in your experience, personality or character. *Impression* is the use of something outside yourself (in our case, music) to change your experience, to make you feel different, to affect you in some way. You switch on the music, and something happens: you are affected, you are "impressed". All of us, whenever we listen to music, are "impressed" in some way, and in this sense impression in itself is not a bad thing at all. But like all the powers which music utilizes, it is open to abuse. What we have to decide is how much we are using music as an impressive force or power in our lives and how much as an expressive force. We also have to decide how much we are using music in church as an impressive force, (in order to make people feel better, change their experience, etc.) and how much we are using it as a vehicle for people to express themselves. For myself, I am in no doubt that we need to be providing a vehicle for people to express what is already inside them. I am also in no doubt that we need to get away from using music as merely a way of changing our feelings, which to me makes it just a brand of entertainment, a temporary relief from reality. Christianity is about discovering reality, not escaping it. Do we really need relief from reality?

Just Like Magic

The magic formula mentality is something which can, if we are not careful, creep in to our use of music. It is actually an occult principle. All magic (black or white) is based on the use of formulas: cast a spell, pronounce a curse, and something will automatically happen. You are tapping into a law which seems to always work, and which you can use at will. Magic seeks through these formulas to gain the power to be able to instantly and automatically change all aspects of life, from outward circumstances to inner feelings and thoughts. With a flick of the fingers, a wave of the wand, the desired effect is produced "out of thin air". All you need is the formula. In an age where so many things are "instant", it sounds like the ideal approach to problem-solving. But in fact, the formulas never deal with the roots of problems. Like an aspirin, they merely deal with the symptoms, and cover over the real problem. What we need to beware of is using music as a kind of magic formula: switch the music on and you'll feel better. There are many means of change, but not all of them are God's way.

Means Of Change

The following illustration may be over-simplifying many cases, but its principles hold true in the majority of circumstances.

If I wake up feeling miserable, I have two basic choices. I can either remain miserable, or I can change. If I want to change, I again have two choices. I can either change myself, or I can use something outside of myself to change me. If I decide to change myself, the first thing I do is question myself: why am I feeling miserable? Perhaps there is a reason, a worry or sorrow, in which case I can address that problem, take it to the Lord, think it through, and face up to it. More often than not it is just feelings, in which case I start to count my blessings, thank God for everything He has done in my life, decide how I can best spend the day getting my mind off myself and serving God and others, and by the time I've been through those thoughts, I've dealt with my problem.

Alternatively, I can use something outside of myself to change my feelings. The hi-fi system is on hand. I simply switch on my favourite track of my favourite album (an action quite unrelated to the real problem), and sure enough, like magic, I start to feel better. But the process of change is entirely different in each case. In the first case, I dealt directly with the problem, found its root, and solved it. In the second instance, I didn't deal with the problem at all. I avoided it, and simply gave myself the equivalent of a spiritual aspirin. That doesn't deal with the problem, it simply makes it go away for a while. It is not real change, only the appearance of it, an illusion. I am relying on something outside of myself; whereas if I deal with the problem myself, I am not relying on any outward props. That, to me, is freedom, and the alternative way is slavery, a bondage which can, if continually used, turn into addiction - the situation where you can no longer manage without the "spiritual aspirin".

It is human nature to always want the circumstances to change. But God usually wants to change *us*, not our circumstances. Why? Because it is always within us that the solution to the problem lies. The Bible also has something to say on this issue in particular connection with music. In one of the few scriptures in the New Testament referring to music, James instructs: "Is any among you afflicted?" (which we can interpret as sad, sorrowful or suffering) "Let him pray. Is any merry? Let him sing psalms." (Jas 5:13)

Notice that James does not say "Is any among you sad? Let him sing a psalm (to cheer himself up)." James advocates tackling the problem directly. According to the Bible, it is when you are happy that you should sing. Why? Because you're expressing how you feel. Happiness is your present experience, and your singing is an *expression* of that, to God and to others.

In the Psalms we catch a glimpse of David's experiences. When he felt cast down, he did not try to cheer himself up with some "magic formula" or instant cure. He examined the problem and questioned himself: "Why art thou cast down, O my soul?" And he went on to encourage himself out of a negative attitude by remembering God: "Hope thou in God, for I shall yet praise Him". (See Ps 42:5,11)

Praise And Worship

Praise is primarily a *consequence* of meeting God, not a *means* of meeting Him. The idea that you can "tap into God's presence" by using praise and worship is very misleading, yet widely prevalent. Christian musicians have discovered that they have power at their disposal, all the powers that music employs; but we must always remember the vital fact that *we do not have the power and presence of God at our disposal*. God cannot be conjured up (which is what magic does). God is not a law that can be tapped into. The Holy Spirit cannot be "invoked" either by words or music. It is all too easy for us to confuse the power of the music with the presence of God, and to adopt formulas, even without realising it, in our mind: "Whenever we play this chorus, God's presence is there" ... "I always feel the anointing when we sing that". It is only one short step further to reverse the formula: "I felt God's anointing when we sang that chorus, so if we sing it again, we will get God's anointing again." I don't think many people would openly advocate such methods; but I do suspect that many people subconsciously think this way. This is a sort of half-way house. It does not go the whole way with the "magic formula" mentality and say, "we will definitely get God's anointing if we reproduce the music that first brought it"; but it is nevertheless rooted in the hope that something at least similar to that might happen. We must shun this type of thinking. There are no foolproof ways of obtaining spiritual results with God. God often responds to the right attitudes in His people (humility, brokenness, integrity, zeal for His name) but He does not respond to music as such, and He never *automatically* responds to anything.

Simon The Sorcerer

Simon of Samaria was used to getting foolproof results. He was a magician, and used the principles of magic to such effect that he was known as "the great power of God" (Acts 8:10). But then he was converted and believed in the Lord. However, when he saw Peter and John lay hands on people in order that they might receive the Holy Spirit, he presumed that they must have control of the power of God, just as he used to have control over spiritual forces by means of magic enchantments and sorcery. But he was making a big mistake. "Give me also this power" he said - and, let it be noted, he had a good motive: "that on whosoever I lay hands, he may receive the Holy Ghost" (Acts 8:19).

Simon was innocent enough, or ignorant. But that is no plea. Ignorance of the truth cannot clear you of a charge of heresy. Peter severely rebuked him, and told him what we all need to know today: the Holy Spirit cannot be bought or controlled at will. Neither dare we use musical atmospheres or manipulative techniques like charms to invoke God's presence, or to manufacture a substitute "anointing". Neither dare we adopt the mentality that says "God is speaking through the music". That's a dangerous and misleading formula. God may speak through people during a time of worship, but He can never be pinned down to formulas. The devil attracts people into the occult with the alluring declaration that formulas do work, that power can be yours, and that there are foolproof ways of getting spiritual results. To back up his claims, he "comes up with the goods" - things do work - until such time as people are in his power, at which time he generally starts to prove that he, not they, had the power all along, and now he not only has power, he has them as well. How important for us not to have any truck with his lying principles - and what an abomination to confuse them with God's principles!

Peter also exposed *wrong attitudes* in Simon's heart. Often wrong attitudes and the desire for magic solutions go together - we want God to work "like magic", but we are unwilling to change our own hearts. We want God to magically alter our *circumstances*, but we don't want to deal with our own *attitudes*. We want to feel God's presence and power, but not His conviction, which might mean that we have to change our lifestyle!

The "praise and worship" situation at present, together with the increased emphasis on times of "ministry" and counselling, is an ideal target for this mentality. We must watch out for it, and not in any way pander to it.

Prayer Aids

The same "magic formula" mentality is sometimes applied to payer. Increasingly, people are using worship tapes as an "aid" to prayer, often as background music to a "quiet time". This really is a dangerous trend. I am convinced that, rather than being an aid to true prayer, putting a tape of Christian music on first thing in the morning is an excuse for not praying - a substitute for prayer.

I once stayed for a few days with an evangelistic organization, sharing a flat with three other Christians. In the morning, the first sounds I heard were music coming from the other people's rooms. This was their private prayer time. I was also praying, and the music disturbed me - but not because of its volume (I could only just hear it when I was in my room) - rather, I just found it exceptionally hard to pray. I couldn't get through to God. I didn't know why. In the end I gave up, and walked down to the open air courtyard of the adjacent building. Suddenly I found I could pray! It was easy to commune with God, far more normal. I was surprised, and wondered why this should be, and then I remembered all the music going on in the flat. I already considered that such use of music in prayer times was really a substitute for prayer; and it makes sense to say that if it is a substitute for true prayer, it is also going to be a hindrance to true prayer. But I'd never experienced the effects of that hindrance until that time. Now I am convinced: this use of music as "impression" banishes the spirit of prayer.

I would certainly appeal to every honest Christian who wants to commune with God and deepen their prayer life - *do without the music in your prayer time*. If you want to know whether it's a "prop" or not, do without it, and see how your prayer time goes. If you find you are completely "dry", then that's a good indication that your spirit is probably just as dry, and your prayer just as unfruitful, when you have the music on. You only "feel better", feel more spiritual, feel as if you are in God's presence. But the presence of music cannot change your prayer life, it can only change your feelings. It is so easy for music to become not an "aid" but a vice, an addiction where, in your mind, "God's presence" and music become inseparable.

We need to learn how to get through to God on our own, without outside help. We need to experience God's presence in our prayer times without the need for music. If God's presence becomes limited to the times when music is playing, whether in church or anywhere else, then alarm bells should be ringing - something is radically wrong.

Chapter 17

New Age Music

Truth exists, only falsehood has to be invented.

George Braque

We have looked at some of the ways in which hypnotic power can have an effect on people playing or listening to heavy rock music. But the same effects can be obtained through quite different sorts of music. The "alternative spirituality" of the New Age is one source that provides an entirely different means of utilising hypnotic power in music. New Agers openly admit that this is the purpose of their music.

The New Age Movement is rooted in many diverse spiritual traditions, some of them Eastern mysticism-related, all of them occult-related. New Agers believe passionately in the spiritual qualities of music. They assert that music is tied up with mankind's spiritual development, and that we are now evolving towards a new understanding of music, a new level of awareness and spirituality which will contribute towards world peace and "universal harmony" (a term deliberately chosen for its musical connotations, as we shall see).

One of the key New Age beliefs is that *sound is spiritual*. This is a popular occult doctrine, and it is opposed to Christianity. The same idea attributes spiritual significance and power to symbols and geometric forms (the reason why witches stand in a pentagram or hexagram to cast a spell, from which comes the word "hex", meaning to bewitch). This is also the reasoning behind the New Age fascination with crystals; spiritual power is attributed to crystals because of their complex geometric structure; their vibrations are connected with the earth's forces and energies.

New Agers believe that the world was created through sound. I recently came across one example of this belief in a prospectus for The London School of Eurythmy. Eurythmy is a little-known art form which uses movement and gesture to express speech and music, based on the work of the occult philosopher Rudolf Steiner. The prospectus begins: "In nearly all ancient traditions the forms of the visible world were held to be created by the Divine Word. Eurythmy is based on the conviction that the sounds of human speech and music have in their own manner and degree something of the same formative power." This is a typical New Age view. Their "religion" is basically pantheistic (God is everything / everything is God), so the idea that God is sound, or that music is part of God, is quite acceptable. (Perhaps this is why the doctrine that Lucifer had instruments built into his body is so prevalent at the moment. The belief that music is a part of Lucifer [the New Age god] is a thought that the devil is probably rather pleased with. We will look further at this theory in Chapter 19). God, in the New Age sense, is "the song of the universe", "the primal sound", "the music of the spheres". As the pseudo-Christian reference to "the Divine Word" above indicates, New Agers like to draw on Christian scriptures to support their arguments about the spiritual nature of sound; "In the beginning was the Word", "He who has ears to hear, let him hear", and "Listen, and your soul shall live" (Is 55:3) are among their favourites.

"Our Whole Being Is Music"

The entire universe, in the New Age view, is like one great piece of music, from the macrocosmic "harmony of the spheres" in the solar system to the microcosmic "music of the sub-atomic particles". New Agers, as you may have gathered from their use of scripture, are prone to taking things out of context and subtly twisting their meaning. They have their own irrational "logic". Music, and all sound, as we have seen, is physical vibration. But they turn the logic around and say that all vibration is sound, or music: so the vibrations and movements of everything from electrons to planets are all a kind of music, all contributing to "the music of the universe".

Drawing from another religion, this time the Sufi mystical tradition within Islam, they quote the writer Hazrat Inayat Khan (the contemporary composer Stockhausen's favourite spiritual reading) who says that the reason human beings are so drawn to music is because "our whole being is music". Our nature and everything around us is music. Our intuitive sense picks up this cosmic "music" and becomes a part of it.

On similar lines, New Agers are fond of using the Eastern mystical technique of chanting mantras. They are keen to point out that it doesn't matter whether you know what your mantra means; the important thing is the sound of the mantra, and the spiritual qualities of that sound.

Sound And Spirit

All of this shows up a very important distinction between the New Age view of music and the Christian view. For Christians, sound does not have any spiritual power or spiritual quality in itself. Spiritual power and quality in music are entirely dependent upon *meaning*; spirit and meaning are inextricably linked. Meaning is given to music by the people playing the music. Divorced from the spirit of the player or composer, the sounds in themselves are dead, meaningless, spiritless. Similarly, words in a dictionary have no power; it is only when a person speaks words that spirit and meaning, and therefore power, is conveyed. Whatever New Agers say, scriptures such as "In the beginning was the Word" have nothing to do with a "primal sound". The Word (*logos* in Greek) was spoken by the personal God; it had meaning, it was an expression of God's thought and Spirit. (*Logos* means, not a sound, or the name of a thing, but *the expression of thought.*) Sounds and words in themselves have no spiritual power.

Expression is the prime purpose of music. Music is for us to express our thoughts and our spirits; it is not about absorption in the vibrations of the universe, but about our expression of what we have experienced and learned. We do not *tap into* the powers of sound and music; we *express* ourselves *through* sound and music, and the power is in our expression, our spirit, our meaning. The music is only a vehicle for our spirit. But if the art of music is about "tapping into universal forces", as New Agers claim, it is the other way around: we become the vehicle for the music, channels for the spiritual power which is in the music. Music is a god which takes possession of us. (As you may remember, the idea that we are a vehicle for music is very prevalent in the classical music world [see Chapter 5]. Perhaps this similarity of thought accounts for the number of contemporary classical composers involved in the New Age.)

Tuning In

New Agers insist that the *way* we listen is very important. They assert that any music, if you listen to it in the right way, can draw you into an experience of altered consciousness, where you become "tuned in" to the spiritual realm, you get on to the "wavelength" of the harmony of the universe. Their use of the word "harmony" is deliberate: they believe that the mathematical relationships of natural harmonics in music are paralleled by the relationships of planets in the solar system.[1] But once again, although the New Age writers use the idea of the "harmony of the universe" to support the doctrine that we are evolving towards oneness with the "universal spiritual forces", they are guilty of subtly twisting a great Christian truth. The facts about natural harmonics actually provide more convincing support for the existence of a personal Creator, a God of order who displays His attributes in His creation. But this is a very different idea from suggesting that the spiritual life and power is found in the creation itself. It is God who has the power, not His creation. New Agers have fallen into the trap outlined by Paul in Romans 1 (verses 18-25) - worshipping the creation instead of the Creator - by attributing spiritual life and power to the creation instead of to the Creator. Tying their beliefs in with a spiritual version of the theory of evolution (a long-time favourite of liberal Christian scholars and world religions alike) they maintain that all creation is evolving towards spiritual unity or "oneness"; the planets are lining up in perfect relationship ("harmonic convergence") and mankind, moving into the astrological "Age of Aquarius", is also evolving onto a new spiritual plane. Where Christians talk of man's need for atonement, New Agers believe we only need "attunement"; all we have to do is to tune into the music of the cosmic vibrations to achieve our spiritual goal, to become fully evolved, fully god-like.

Brainwaves And Enlightenment

The spiritual enlightenment sought by New Agers comes in the form of altered states of consciousness. Neurologists have identified different types of brainwave patterns of varying frequencies. *Beta* waves are the normal wave patterns of the brain of a fully conscious person; such a person is said to be in a "Beta state" of consciousness. *Alpha* waves are slightly slower, leading to a change in consciousness approximating to a light state of meditation. John Lennon (quoted in Chapter 9) said that he used to "trance out into alpha", in which state he experienced hallucinations. *Delta* and *Theta* wave patterns produce deeper states of meditation; consciousness is radically altered. In the deeper states of altered consciousness, the rational part of the brain is effectively switched off; you lose control of your rational faculties, and the subconscious takes over.

Our medical knowledge of brainwave patterns and altered states of consciousness can give us some insights into hypnotic effects and the way they can be induced. By "locking in" to these altered states, New Agers, along with the exponents of many religions and mystical traditions down the centuries, hope to achieve enlightenment and blend into the "harmony of the universe", becoming one with all creation. Specially composed music, along with all sorts of other "sense stimulants", help the meditational process along.

Before Randall Baer was converted to Christianity, he was a leading New Age practitioner. One of his achievements was the design and construction of a special room filled with objects and experiences specifically aimed at inducing a trance-state in the recipient. The room (called an "Ascension Chamber") contained hundreds of crystals and pyramids, all designed to create a "spiritual energy field", complemented by the use of lasers, psychedelic light shows, video, aromatic agents, and mystical New Age music - swirling, gentle, super-relaxing music - quite the opposite of heavy rock. But the music, and everything else, was purposely created to help induce a hypnotic state. Baer confirmed that the effects on people using this "healing temple" were startling, including mystical experiences, altered states of consciousness, and out-of-body experiences.[2]

Trance-Inducing Music

The New Age insistence that any music can bring about an altered state of consciousness, if it is listened to in the right way, is supported by evidence. One ethno-musicologist has travelled the world doing research into trance-inducing music, trying to find out what common ground there was in the music which brought about trance states in the religious/mystical rituals of various cultures. His conclusions were that *there was no one musical element that had to be present.* The musical styles, techniques and devices that brought about trance states were remarkably diverse. It seemed to be more to do with the listeners' expectations and receptivity.

People do indeed testify of "spiritual experiences" happening to them while listening to many different sorts of music. A classical violinist told of an experience he had while playing a symphony by Mahler: he felt himself to be lifted out of his chair, and "soared above the stage while playing the music". He had an "out-of-body experience", well known to New Agers and students of meditation world-wide.

Certainly the emphasis on the importance of "listening in the right way", or receptivity, seems to be a crucial element in determining whether "spiritual experiences" result. But much New Age music is purpose-designed to help induce altered states. Is there any danger in listening to this sort of music? Can there be harmful spiritual effects? I think the real danger is that you could be "opening yourself up" without realising it. We need to consider very carefully our purpose and object in listening to music. We should be constantly in control of our mind and consciousness - not pursuing an experience which will take us off into another realm, a "super-relaxed state", a "spiritual experience", an ego trip, or anything like that. Music's true purpose is not to take us away from reality, but to express reality as it is. However, the idea that music's purpose is to take us into an experience "beyond ourselves" is so prevalent, in one form or another, that it has become a part of our whole way of thinking; and because of this, unless we are careful, we run the risk of unconsciously putting ourselves in a place of receptivity to effects that might well be harmful.

The New Age - A Triple Counterfeit

There are three points to make about the New Age before we leave the subject. The first is that it is a counterfeit of the true "New Age" - the reign of Christ on earth. The devil only counterfeits God's works and plans. The Psalms (often called "the worship book of the Bible"), have an important prophetic significance in this regard. Many of the praises that resound in the Psalms point not to this age but forward to the coming of the Messiah in glory. The association of music and the "true New Age" is very clear. So the importance of music in the counterfeit New Age is hardly surprising. But "the end is not yet"; antichrist will bring the counterfeit kingdom to a head before Christ is revealed and brings in the real Kingdom of God. Then it will be the time to celebrate; then the psalms will have their fulfilment. Watchman Nee, with typically astute observation, noted that the only "Hallelujahs" in the New Testament are in the book of Revelation, in the song which proclaims the destruction of Babylon and the coming of Christ's Kingdom (Rev 19:1-4).

Secondly, the New Age is anything but new. Eclectic in the extreme, it draws its doctrines and practices from hundreds of different sources, ancient, medieval and post-Enlightenment, Buddhist, Taoist, humanist and animist, religious, artistic and political. The idea of "the harmony of the spheres", for example, is first found in the writings of

Pythagoras (c.550 B.C.) and was developed in the Middle Ages by Boethius (c.500 A.D.), then became the focus of attention again in the works of Johannes Kepler (1571-1650). The idea that sounds possess power is found in most primitive religions and in Indian mysticism, but again it has later developments: in the 3rd century A.D. the Roman philosopher Plotinus "interpreted music as a mystic and occult power" [Harvard Dictionary of Music], and his ideas were greatly influential in the Italian Renaissance (15th Century). And so on. The weave of threads tied together in the New Age Movement is a compendium of occult, humanist and antichristian thought, much of which has formed the foundation of our common human understanding of the arts. The New Age teachers have, therefore, a substantial ideological and philosophical base upon which to rest their arguments.

Truth And Lies

Lastly, a word of explanation. We have pointed out that New Age teaching and technique can be traced back to occult roots. But it is important to realise that these teachings and practices are not wrong or false because they are occultic. It is the other way around - they are only occultic because they are false and wrong in the first place. It is the devil, the master of falsehood and deceit, "a liar from the beginning", who is the author of the false idea that sounds and geometric forms have spiritual power. The so-called "spiritual experience" of the trance-state or altered consciousness shuts off the rational part of the brain, allowing the subconscious to have free reign and opening up people's spirits - whereupon the devil can infiltrate into the mind, because the natural defences are broken down. Our spiritual-psychological-physical make-up includes protective mechanisms designed to guard our spirit. When we lose that protection, we are opened up to the possibility of possession. The devil is intent on getting our defences down, and one of his ways of doing that is to begin by telling an alluring lie: "Sounds have spiritual power". In fact, once people are "opened up", it is evil spirits, not music, that exercise the spiritual power over them, because spiritual power only comes from spirits, be they men or demons. (Likewise, spiritualism, claiming to bring people into contact with dead relatives or friends, instead brings then into contact with demons in disguise. No spiritualist ever contacted a dead person, only a living demon.) All the so-called spiritual powers or forces that are attributed to "things" are lies of the devil. The devil makes occultism from falsehoods; all occult systems are based on untruths.

Notes

1. An explanation of the natural laws of harmonics can be found in the Appendix at the end of this book.
2. Randall Baer, *Inside the New Age Nightmare* (Huntington House, 1989), pp 49-50.

Chapter 18

Hypnotism In The Church

We live at the mercy of a malevolent world. A sound, a mere disturbance of the air, sinks into our very soul sometimes.

Joseph Conrad

Has New Age music infiltrated the church? Unfortunately, it has. I have personally witnessed a Christian leader from a well respected evangelical charismatic group using New Age cassettes as a background to corporate prayer and meditation times, supposedly, again, to create "an atmosphere conducive to prayer". The leader in question didn't know the tape he had chosen was New Age, although he ought to have known. It was called "The Fairy Ring", and its sleeve notes described it as an aid to relaxation, soothing the mind, and so on. Did it have any hypnotic effect? Did it induce altered states of consciousness in the listeners? It probably did! Clearly it was designed to by whoever made the tape. And this Christian leader was using it in the way it was designed to be used. So it would be no surprise if it did have all the desired effects, relaxing people and soothing their minds.

Moreover, some Christians are now suggesting that altered states of consciousness are a normal part of charismatic faith.[1] Now it may well be that when God moves by His Holy Spirit, people do enter different states of consciousness. The apostle Peter "fell into a trance" while praying (Acts 10:10). But what God does and what we do are two very different things. My concern arises when we try to duplicate the works of God by inducing altered states of consciousness - particularly, using music to create a "spiritual atmosphere". This then becomes another formula, one more "technique" for entering the spiritual realm. It works - that is, it has effects - but what does it all have to do with the genuine presence of God, or with Christian worship?

I have also been at a church meeting where the chorus time started with a fast, loud drum beat, which drove the whole "worship" incessantly for about ten minutes. That may not sound a long time, but when it is non-stop, fast, driving music completely dominated by rhythm, it seems interminable! Eventually it slowed down; but that is the only time I have personally felt so disturbed in my spirit in a church that I wondered whether I ought to leave before any harm was done to me. I was afraid of the subconscious effects it might be having, because I didn't really feel in control of my mind with the incessant pounding of the music going on.

It didn't seem to disturb anybody else. They were all dancing, clapping, well into it. They were used to it. So I knew I couldn't question any of them about it. Once you become accustomed to this kind of thing, you're blinded to the power of its effects, and you take them for granted. It becomes natural and normal - the same process that we noted concerning the acceptance of new musical styles.

The Subversion Of The Mind

At this point you might reasonably ask the question: what exactly is the nature of the hypnosis we have been talking about? After all, people don't come out of rock concerts looking "tranced out", neither do they obey the first thing that is suggested to them by their friends. They seem to be fully themselves. But with hypnosis, the activity is subliminal and subconscious, and auto-suggestion is the key. A message is implanted into your subconscious when you are in an "opened up" or receptive state, and there are "triggers" that set off the implanted suggestion in your mind. Even the auto-suggestion happens subconsciously, without you being aware of it. You appear normal to others, you feel normal yourself, your mind seems to function normally.

You have probably heard the stories surrounding the introduction of "subliminal advertising" into cinemas. A picture of a product was flashed onto the screen for a split second - too short a time for the eye to see it, but time enough for the brain to subconsciously register it. When popcorn was advertised in cinemas in this way, everything about the audience remained normal - until the interval, when popcorn appeared on sale. That was the trigger. Suddenly everybody was queuing for popcorn! And to them, that was only a normal desire; not a blinding urge, which would have seemed abnormal. They just fancied some popcorn. The only remarkable thing was that they all fancied it at the same time!

This basically illustrates the process which happens with any hypnotic effect. It doesn't leave you in a trance. The hypnotic medium, whether it is a flash frame on a cinema screen, a piece of music, or a swinging watch, is only for the purpose of opening you up, so that the real operation can be performed - the implanting in your subconscious mind of perhaps only one little statement. The job of the music or flashing picture is accomplished; you remain, to all appearances, quite normal and unaware of any change. The change, indeed, is not immediately apparent. It often works out slowly in people's lifestyles; a change in desire or will - it might be an increased desire for alcohol or certain foods, or perhaps a new fascination for the occult, perhaps a recurring sexual fantasy, perhaps an urge to listen to more music, or different sorts of music. Or it could be a change in attitude; a new rebelliousness, or restlessness, or an onset of depression, or "bad nerves". Often it is simply a thought or idea to do with general attitudes, ethos, world-view, morals and values - something that changes the whole way you think.

As Dave Crosby remarked,[2] the sort of ideas that rock singers preached into the subconscious minds of their young audiences did its work with amazing success. It removed them from their parents' world, and their parents' values, very effectively - the most subtle and effective form of kidnapping available. The "suggestion" could be anything. Only occasionally does it result in serious crime, as appears to be the case with Charles Manson, who was heavily influenced by The Beatles' "White Album" (the lyrics of which are full of witchcraft language), or Richard Ramirez, the "Night Stalker" murderer of the west coast of America, who was obsessed by satanic themes in the music of heavy metal band AC/DC, and in particular their album "Highway to Hell". In those cases, the links between music and harmful effect are obvious. But in most cases, the link is far less obvious, and goes largely unnoticed. It is a hidden, secret, subversive work. When the implanted suggestion is triggered and takes effect, the resultant change is usually blamed on something else, or simply remains unexplained. How many parents, exasperated at the inexplicable behaviour of their teenager, confess, "I just don't know what's got into him!"? It is quite possible that something has indeed "got into him" - a subliminal suggestion, implanted into the subconscious mind through the mind-opening techniques inherent in the power of music. But how would the unsuspecting parent ever guess that?

"Opening People Up" - Fair Play?

Jimi Hendrix, as we have seen, declared that he used music to "open people up" so that he could "preach into their subconscious" what he wanted to say. We would all agree that to take advantage of people by "preaching into their subconscious" without them knowing what is happening, is a gross abuse of power. Subliminal advertising was banned because it was an abuse of power that worked remarkably well. The power of what is "preached into the subconscious" is very real, and very effective.

If we as Christians want to have our minds filled with truth, God's word, and right attitudes, might it not be legitimate to "open ourselves up" through music to receive truth from God, via the preacher or direct from God's Spirit - truth that would then lodge deep in our subconscious, and provide a solid spiritual foundation for our lives? In fact this is already happening. There are now "scripture tapes" available which are produced specifically as relaxation aids, the aim being to brainwash yourself with the scriptures. You can play the tape last thing at night, so that your mind is subconsciously filled with the scriptures as you are going to sleep. And for many years there has been in some Christian circles a practice of "positive affirmation" "speaking out" scriptures, repeating them over and over to yourself through the day, with the aim that the words will embed themselves into your spirit. In fact, there is little to distinguish this from brainwashing techniques.

The Brain And The Mind

It may be argued that there is nothing wrong with brainwashing as such. Most education is, after all, actually a form of brainwashing, in the sense that it is basically repeating information over and over until it becomes "programmed" into the brain. But Christianity is not just a form of education; it is not about learning information and repeating it by rote; it is not about knowing scriptures and being able to trot them out "parrot-fashion". That would put the scriptures on the same level as multiplication tables or, worse, the slogans of totalitarian states. Christianity is not about re-programming the brain, it is about renewing the mind, and that is a very different thing.

This needs a word of explanation. The brain and the mind are not the same. The brain is part of our *physical* make-up; but the mind is part of our *spiritual* make-up. The brain is like a computer, and can be programmed; but the brain cannot think for itself any more than a computer can. It is the mind that thinks, the mind that is "sound" or otherwise, the mind that is renewed, not the brain. A brainwashed or re-programmed brain automatically functions in certain ways, regardless of the person's will. But a renewed mind is always under the person's control, both in the process of renewal and in the resultant renewed state. The person with a renewed mind thinks for himself, intelligently; the brainwashed person doesn't have to do any personal, original thinking about the subjects in which he has been brainwashed, because his brain is already programmed; the thinking has been done, the answers are already there, and are never questioned.

Direct Access

As Christians we cannot use or legitimize hypnotic techniques, simply because they are part of the devil's way of working, not God's. Only God has the key of direct access to our spirits. The Creator made man's spirit with natural physical and psychological defences. Our reasoning capability, the instinctive reflexes and shut-off mechanisms in the brain, are there to protect the spirit, just as other devices protect the body by sending warning signals in the form of pain when the body is in danger. God intended that only He should be able to access our spirits directly.

Not surprisingly, the devil also wants access to our spirits. However, he can't get in directly, so he has to find another way. One of his ways is to attack the natural defences and safeguards that God has placed there, by anaesthetizing the brain, shutting down those defence mechanisms and getting in to your mind, thus gaining access to your spirit via your brain. Then the "preaching" the devil does is the exact equivalent of what a man is told under hypnosis. A hypnotized man does things he is told to do - but he is not a willing co-operator. His will does not come into it. (Of course, he was willing to be hypnotized in the first place. In that sense he is a willing co-operator. But once he is hypnotized he is not co-operating willingly any longer - he has surrendered his will to the control of another.) A hypnotized man will do things he would never normally do. He is not in control. That is the essential point. God always wants us in control. He wants us to willingly choose His way. The devil, on the other hand, doesn't care how he gets you; willingly or unwillingly, consciously or subconsciously. His followers are programmed, brainwashed, yet they don't realise it. Jesus' followers have this distinction: they have a *sound mind* (2 Tim 1:7). They can always think straight; they are always in control. It is vital to us as Christians that we do not risk surrendering that privilege. Our mind, spirit and body belong to God: the devil must not be allowed to infiltrate them by his subtle means. We have to watch what we listen to!

Notes

1. Dr. Patrick Dixon, in *Signs of Revival* (Kingsway, 1995) devotes several pages to justifying this idea from a medical and spiritual viewpoint (pp. 258-279).
2. Quoted in Chapter 7.

Chapter 19

The Lucifer Doctrine

The devil has a whole system of theology and philosophy ... as might be expected, the moral theology of the devil grants an altogether unusual amount of importance to - the devil.

Thomas Merton

In recent years a new and intriguing doctrine has been gaining popularity in various Christian circles. Its basic premise is that Satan (who is generally identified with "Lucifer" of Isaiah 14), was the worship leader in heaven. The justification for this view is the prophecy of Ezekiel 28, which refers to the King of Tyre (also understood to be a "type" of Satan) having "workmanship of tabrets and pipes" prepared in him. This is taken to mean that he had musical instruments "built in to his body".[1] However, the whole doctrine is extremely shaky, for several reasons. Firstly, it is bad practice to base any doctrine on allegorical prophecy. Secondly, the identification of Satan with Lucifer is not at all certain; some Bible scholars, for instance, believe that "Lucifer" in Isaiah 14 refers to the antichrist, not the devil. Thirdly, the words translated "tabrets and pipes" in the Authorized Version are not definitive translations by any means: the New American Standard Version, for instance, translates Ezekiel 28:13 as: "The workmanship of your *settings and sockets* was in you ..." relegating "*tambourines and flutes*" to an alternative marginal reading. But even if the scriptures in Isaiah and Ezekiel do refer to Satan, and even if he did have musical instruments built into his body, it is still wildly speculative to deduce that he was "the worship leader in heaven". A tenuous doctrine at best! -

which makes one wonder how it ever came about - or, more importantly, *why* it ever came about. It is interesting to note that this teaching has become popular at a time of massive increase in the importance of music in church, when the term "worship" seems to have become almost synonymous with "singing in church".

Hidden Principles Behind The Doctrine

The reason I am so unhappy about this doctrine is because of what it goes on to deduce: firstly, that "Satan hates to hear the worship of God". This seems true enough, on the face of it; but it goes wrong in equating worship with music, and worship actually has nothing to do with music, any more than your bedside has to do with prayer. You may use music in your worship, and you may kneel at your bedside to pray; but that is as far as the identification can go in either instance. Satan may well hate to hear or see true worship of God, but he does not necessarily hate music, or even everything that goes by the name "praise and worship music". Indeed, one of the more sobering suggestions in this book is that he may be quite keen on some of it.

Secondly, the teachers who propound the "Lucifer the worship leader" doctrine say that Christians now need to "redeem" worship/music, because it was in Satan's/Lucifer's charge when he fell, and it needs to be "restored." How? By Christians incorporating all sorts of different music styles into their worship of God.[2] Their scriptural basis for the "restoration of music" argument here shifts to James' quote of an Old Testament prophecy in Acts 15:16 :- "After this I will return, and will build again the tabernacle of David which is fallen down". The inference taken from this is that David had the musicians and choir taking on a role of new importance in the tabernacle worship (see 1 Chr 15:16-24, 23:5). Whether "the tabernacle of

David" means "the tabernacle in the time of David" is a matter of interpretation; but in any case the context of James' words has nothing to do with music or worship, either in Acts or in the Old Testament scripture from which it was taken (Amos 9:11).[3]

Music is even, these teachers declare, a key to revival; once music is redeemed and restored for God, it becomes an agent for bringing revival. But against this it has to be said that although praise and worship music is often a *consequence* of revival, it is not a *means* of revival. Prayer, seeking God and repentance seem to be the scriptural and historical keys to revival, not music.

"Spiritual Warfare" - Formulas For Power

Another favourite theme of the proponents of this new doctrine is an emphasis on praise as warfare, and music as a kind of ammunition with which to defeat the enemy. Here reference is often made to the story of King Jehoshaphat sending singers out at the front of the army, whereupon the Lord set the Ammonites and Moabites fighting amongst themselves, and Israel had victory without even needing to fight (2 Chronicles 20:21,22). But this was an isolated incident, and was no more intended to constitute a "formula for victory" than walking round the walls of Jericho seven times. The obvious danger here is the "magic formula mentality" described in Chapter 16 coming into play. In this case, it takes the form of: "If we praise, the devil flees". He may well do. Or he may well not. But once praise is equated in our minds with warfare, it is a short step to regarding praise choruses as being as automatically effective as a bullet from a gun. However, we have no such guarantees or foolproof formulas for success in Christianity. This teaching is the musical equivalent of believing that the name of Jesus has some magical power of itself, or that every time we use the "scriptural formula" of "binding and loosing" it will automatically happen as we say. That's not how it works! Our weapons are not formulas or "things" at all, as Sceva's sons found out to their cost when they tried to exercise their deliverance ministry with the formula "In the name of Jesus" (see Acts 19:13-16). If you want a powerful weapon against the devil, there is one - a holy life and a holy mind - and we will be examining the positive use of music for God, and its relation to our spiritual walk and our relationship with God, in Part III.

Doctrines of Devils

The whole doctrine of "redeeming music" and of Satan having been the worship leader in heaven is actually a red herring, a fanciful concoction from the devil's own publicity department, designed to divert our minds from God and onto the devil. It encourages unhealthy misunderstandings about spiritual warfare, it appeals to the "magic formula" mentality, it tends to identify worship with music, and it ascribes more power to the devil than he actually has. The devil is happy enough for us to think that praise and worship music is an "automatic weapon" against him, if he can encourage us to concentrate on generating more praise and worship music, at the expense of developing a holy life and a holy mind.

Perhaps the most notable feature of this doctrine is that it all centres around the devil; and any doctrine which does that must be regarded with the greatest suspicion. One of the devil's prime aims is deviation - to get us off the track, divert us from God's purpose and prevent us from getting to the place of real power where his dark kingdom would be truly threatened.

Notes

1. These thoughts are to be found in LaMar Boschman's book *The Rebirth of Music* [Revival Press, 1980]. His is only one among a growing number of books promoting the same ideas.
2. This doctrine is clearly implied in Stephen Bennett's prophecy (quoted in Chapter 15).
3. Amos does actually have a few things to say about music earlier in his prophecy, but as they are rather negative and judgmental things, they tend to be passed over by musicians and "Lucifer Doctrine" teachers alike! The passages are 6:5 (which I have quoted in Chapter 24) and the following:
   "*I hate, I despise your feast days, and I will not smell in your solemn assemblies. Though ye offer me burnt offerings and your meat offerings, I will not accept them: neither will I regard the peace offerings of your fat beasts. Take thou away from me the noise of thy songs: I will not hear the melody of thy viols. But let judgment run down as waters, and righteousness as a mighty stream.*" (5:21-24)

Chapter 20

Image

The media have created, and belong to, a world of fantasy, the more dangerous because it purports to be, and is largely taken as being, the real world ... Now we, the legatees of Christendom, are in turn succumbing to fantasy ... the effect of the media at all levels is to draw people away from reality, which means away from Christ, and into fantasy.

Malcolm Muggeridge

20th Century culture thrives on image. Some sections of society are almost wholly dependent on it. Image influences us all, and the arts and the media have conspired to make us an image-conscious society.

What do I mean by "image"? To illustrate, we need to digress from music for a minute and look at an obvious example - fashion. Clothes have always been status symbols, but these days the status that fashion bestows upon us is not primarily to do with wealth or position in the social hierarchy. Fashion today serves a deeper psychological purpose. Through it we make a statement about our values, our personality, our opinions and allegiances, even our way of thinking. That's where the concept of a "fashion statement" springs from. The clothes themselves are only half the story. The important thing is what the clothes signify, what they stand for. Through the fashions we adopt, we create an "image" for ourselves. The image we create is basically determined by the way we would like others to see us. This image, then, is not just physical; in fact it is primarily a psychological thing.

The Source Of The Image

The ideas and inspirations for these sorts of images come from the fashion houses and from the media. They don't usually come from the general public, the people who wear the fashions. In other words, we don't actually create the image, we just (literally!) fit into an image that is created for us. Through the immensely powerful influence of the media, advertisers are enabled to elaborate on the meaning of the image behind the fashion, so that the clothes come to stand for a whole system of values, an entire way of thinking, a complete ethos. Because the media reach the whole of society, the "image" attached to a particular fashion can be made very clear. By associating the fashion with certain people, situations and values, the language and meaning of the image swiftly becomes universally understood.

We can see in the example of fashion how image has become an increasingly sophisticated and important factor in society. Eventually the image becomes absorbed into the mainstream of society, and then it ceases to be an up-to-date statement: new trends take over and become the dominant statements. But that does not detract from the power and effect of the original image. It may have long since become "normal" and acceptable, but society has changed because of it, and perhaps changed dramatically.

Two relatively recent examples are the fashion of long hair for men, which began with the hippy movement, and that of short hair for women, which gained popularity in the feminist movement. Scripture says that long hair is a shame to a man, but glory for a woman, and vice versa (see 1 Cor 11:14-15); and both the hippies' long hair and the feminists' short hair were in part deliberate reactions against the current (nominally Christian) social convention. But now that the sixties revolution and Women's Lib have been well absorbed into mainstream culture, we do not think of a man with long hair as a rebel or an outcast of society; nor do we suppose that every woman with short hair is making a feminist statement. Both the physical fashion and the image or statement behind it have now become more acceptable and normal, and we take them for granted; but, of course, that does not justify their point of view or make it right.

Become The Person You Want To Be

The media have total control over the images created by fashion, and, partly because of this fact, the vital element in fashion has gradually become the image itself. The clothes are only a means to an end - the means of attaining the image. Wear the clothes, and you take on the image. The image may be one of sophistication, elegance and tradition, appealing to "refined tastes"; or it may be directed at those who want to appear cool and "with it". There are thousands of different images to choose from; you just pick one to suit yourself.

The advertisers' aim is to hook us on the image they are selling; but, naturally enough, they are anxious to not put it in those terms. Instead, they put the emphasis on our personal choice and freedom. "What you wear says a lot about you", they say, implying that they are giving us the opportunity to express our own personality through the choice of fashions they present. This is a great hoax, but it is something that lies at the foundation of what image is all about. It is true that some people do express their personality in their dress; but these people are not usually fashion-conscious, rather the opposite - they have no interest in following trends or adopting images, only in expressing their personality. Such "expressers" are usually secure and self-confident people; they don't tend to worry about what others think of them, and are generally less concerned with fashion, because they recognize that it is their inner personality, rather than their outward clothing, that is the key to successful relationships, friendships and social behaviour. They have no need of fashion "props" in order to impress people or bolster up their personality by creating an "image" for themselves.

Wish-Fulfilment

At its root, the whole concept of image is a form of "impression"; a kind of wish-fulfilment, whereby we take on the characteristics of what we would like to be and how we would like to be thought of by others. Rather than expressing ourselves as we are, fashion actually presents us with the opportunity to hide behind an image, an image we are convinced is successful (because we've seen it in the adverts, and it has convinced us!) In this way, we gradually come to believe that we really are made more appealing, admirable or trendy by what we wear. We feel we have become the image by clothing ourselves in its garb.

Of course, we have not "become" anything at all, only slaves to fashion trends. Image is pure fantasy, a gigantic game controlled by the fashion business through the channels of the mass media, offering us (for a price) the chance to become someone other than we really are.

It hardly needs saying that fashion is only one example of the vast influence of image in society. Image is of vital importance to people who are in the public eye, because they are so dependent on the media. For this reason, be they politicians, businessmen or entertainers, they are all dependent on image for success, whether it is to win an election, launch a new product or sell more records. The vast sums of money poured into advertising bear witness to this; and the sheer volume of research and painstaking work that goes into getting an advert to convey exactly the right image is an extraordinary testimony to the importance - and the success - of image in society today.

The Paradox Of Image

Because advertisers depend so much upon image to convey their message through the media, the media in turn have come more and more to represent fantasy rather than truth. Reality, for us as "consumers", is increasingly being smothered by fantasy. In fact, the fantasy of image has become a major force in society today. We are too often willing to believe and follow what people tell us because we are drawn by the appeal of its image - even if what they are telling us stands in stark opposition to the truth.

This is demonstrated clearly in the advertising of consumer goods. Marlboro cigarettes, to take just one example, ran a long poster advertising campaign which always featured a cowboy. Those adverts were as near as you could get to pure image. They had nothing to do with reality, and bore no relevance at all to how good Marlboro cigarettes are. The cowboy was often pictured resting, calmly surveying the serene, sunlit plains. It was an image of "a moment of pure satisfaction". (That, of course, was the hook, the subliminal message - Marlboro cigarettes will give you that "moment of pure satisfaction"). Yet this image of idyllic contentment was presented to people hooked on nicotine, people who will go and buy a packet of cigarettes because they need it to calm their nerves and help them get through the day.

The image is meticulously contrived to say exactly the right thing. The cowboy is carefree, yet secure; alone, yet content and problem-free. He is certainly not worried about going into hospital for a major operation, or depressed because his wife has just left him, or distraught because his kids are on drugs. He doesn't belong to the real world. If he did, it wouldn't be fantasy, the image wouldn't work, and it certainly wouldn't sell any cigarettes. People follow the fantasy and pursue the attainment of the image by buying the product. (They would probably never admit this, but it is true - the success of the advertising itself proves it. Cigarette manufacturers would never spend millions of pounds of their precious profits on these sorts of advertisements if they didn't work.) The reality of our daily lives is constantly inspired and influenced by these fantasies. If the media can be called a popular extension of the arts, then life, for us, reflects art.

Image And Idolatry

The media have created the role models for the new images we worship. The fact that the word "image" is also used to describe pagan idols or false gods is not a coincidence. In both cases, the image is something we serve, follow and worship, and in both cases we derive our value system from the images we serve.

The 20th century idols are not found in religious temples; they belong to the new cathedrals and shrines of media-driven consumerism - the shopping malls, the advertising hoardings, the magazines, the television, and the album covers. Society's "saints" and role models are living models - fashion models, TV, film and pop stars (who, if their earnings are anything to go by, have been elevated almost to the status of gods - at least for as long as their looks last, and their image suits the purpose). 20th century western culture is not dissimilar to the pagan society of ancient Greece, when there were thousands of gods to choose from. You simply worshipped your favourite, the one that suited you best and attracted you the most.

The Musical Image

We have spent some time discussing the concept of image. We have seen that image is *fantasy*, it is vastly *influential*, it is a form of *impression* and a form of *idolatry*, and it pervades every area of western society and thought. But how does it relate to music and Christianity?

There are in fact clear links. The powers for which music is such an ideal medium include all of the above listed elements - fantasy, impression, idolatry, and powerful influence - from which we can deduce that image and music must be closely related. In fact, as we shall see, image is a vital element in the appeal and success of music. We know that there are fashions and trends in music; but it is perhaps not so obvious that these trends are always part of an image. It's "in" to go along with the new image; it's fashionable to "get into" a new musical style. But just what are you going along with when you get into a new style? What exactly is the "musical image" that appeals so much? What are the values behind it? Is it simply a matter of musical preference and taste, or is there more to it than that? I believe that there certainly is more to it, and in order to understand what is going on, we need to look at a concept closely related to image - *myth*.

Image And Myth

Myths always have a place among the basic foundations of the value systems of human societies. A myth is a "fiction", legend or fantasy (often a narrative, sometimes loosely based on historical fact), which embodies certain important social or moral concepts and values. The "fiction" itself is not meant to be taken seriously or literally, and its heroes are not usually to be regarded as real people; it is the concepts and values embodied in the myth that are the serious part. The myths that have stood the test of time are those which have embodied the values that civilization holds most dear, and those which best express mankind's present condition, consciousness, hopes, dreams and fears. Sometimes myths exist without having a prominent or specific "fiction" attached to them. They are simply value systems and ideologies which lie, often quite unknown to us, at the root of many of the things we see and hear, the way we think, and the lifestyles we lead.

In the 20th century, the media have become the purveyors of the new mythology. Far broader in its scope and influence than advertising, fashion or consumerism, this new myth encompasses our whole civilization, and is the primary source of our value system and way of thought. Our whole culture is based on it.

The huge "fiction" which forms the basis of the modern myth is the fantasy of image. I suppose we all know in the back of our minds that the adverts bear precious little relation to reality. However, the point is not that we literally believe what the "fictitious" adverts tell us; it's that we believe in, or are drawn to, the values and ideas contained in that image. Because these values are presented to us in the form of an image, they appeal far more strongly to us. The values are not explicitly stated, so we are often not consciously aware of them (for we are meant to accept them, not think about them); rather, they are subtly fed into our subconscious through the images presented to us by the media in all its manifestations - television, radio, film, music, theatre, the visual arts, literature, magazines and newspapers, to name only a few.

Sociologist and author Alvin Toffler explains the way in which images incorporate values: "Every person carries within his head a mental model of the world - a subjective representation of external reality. This model consists of tens upon tens of thousands of images. These may be as simple as a mental picture of clouds scudding across the sky, or they may be abstract inferences about the way things are organized in society. We may think of this mental model as a fantastic internal warehouse, an image emporium in which we store our inner portraits of Twiggy, Charles de Gaulle or Cassius Clay, along with such sweeping propositions as 'Man is basically good' or 'God is dead'."[1] We must be alert to these sorts of "sweeping propositions", because many such implicit values find their way, through image, into both music and Christianity.

Music And Myth

We have already seen something of the myth behind classical music. It is this myth, with its concomitant values, based on fantasy and supported by image, which actually gives musical styles much of their power to influence society. The myth behind classical music is based on the fantasy of the nobility of man, the greatness of man and the glory of man. Very rarely are these values stated explicitly in the music, but they silently pervade it all the way through (and perhaps this is most grossly exemplified by the high class, ultra-dignified "white tie and tails" dress still adopted by most orchestras).

The same principle holds true for all styles of music. As we saw in Chapter 8, every style has its own ethos, a distinctive spirit and value system at the back of it; the music itself is, in a sense, only the "front" for that value system and way of thinking. Music is an eminently suitable vehicle for conveying myth because of its utilization of the subconscious, and because it is a medium for the same influential spiritual powers as image (fantasy, impression, evocation). Image can have the same effects as music (psychological and emotional manipulation, subliminal auto-suggestion) and produce the same results (brainwashing, addiction, idolatry). Music and myth work readily together - we only have to think of the number of operas based on myths and legends to see that - because both feed and fire the imagination so powerfully.

Myth And Religion

Myths form the basis of many religions; even Christianity has not been immune from attempts by modernist scholars to mythologize the historical evidence for Jesus and re-interpret Christianity as a myth-based religion - merely a value system based on a fiction. This suits the purpose of these "liberal theologians", who would rather not have to take Jesus' unique and exclusive claims too seriously; it enables them to pick and choose the scriptures they like, line them up with the values of other religions and help to foster a pluralistic, broad-minded, universal "faith". But the truth of the matter is that Christianity and religion are very different things. Strangely - or perhaps it is not so strange, if we take into account the strategies of "the prince of this world" - many of the values of the myths which form the foundations of religions are also the values of the 20th century myth promoted by the media through "image". And here is the crunch - these values are all opposed to Christianity. A comparison of the basic values of religion with the values of Christianity highlights the fact that the two systems are irreconcilably opposed, and also shows up the similarity between the values of religion and those of the "modern myth":

1. Christianity is based on historical fact, substantiated by evidence. The historical facts of Jesus' life are of crucial importance to Christianity. Religion is often based on myths and legends which are not intended to be taken as fact. Even when historical facts are involved, they tend not to be the important element in the religion. The dates and events of Buddha's life are not the essential aspects of Buddhism; the only important things are the values that Buddha taught. The same is true of most religions.

2. A vital aspect of Christianity is that it is a revelation. God has revealed Himself to us. The only "mysteries" in the Bible are revealed mysteries. But mystery is one of the essential aspects of religion. Without mystery, religion loses much of its power.

3. Christianity declares that Jesus Christ is the only way to God. Religions say that there are many ways to God, each as good as the other.

4. Christianity says that God is a literal person. Religions tend to say that God is an impersonal force, like goodness or love or beauty. For them, the idea of God as a person, with whom one can have a personal relationship, is outdated; this God "is dead". Religion has "evolved" beyond the "primitive" idea of the personal God.

5. Christianity says that man cannot save himself; he is inwardly corrupt. Religion will not have this, and declares that man is innately noble; that though he may choose to do evil, he nevertheless has the seeds of his own salvation, even his own godhood, inside him. Many religions teach that "you are God", and focus on man's inner potential for spiritual enlightenment. It is fascinating to note that the two "image-slogans" arbitrarily singled out by Alvin Toffler in *Future Shock* (quoted earlier) were "Man is basically good" and "God is dead" - expressing exactly the values of this myth. (Toffler, a non-Christian, was writing in 1970.)

6. Christianity has moral absolutes. God's moral law holds good for every circumstance and society. Religion is more free, and tends to adapt the rules for different ages and situations. Some religions teach a kind of moral relativism. (Moral relativism is the idea that morals can never be absolute; that no-one can dictate universally what is right and wrong; the emphasis is placed on the individual person's freedom and responsibility to decide for themselves what is right and wrong, relative to situations as they occur). This is a fundamental doctrine of the 20th century myth, the worldview fostered by the media which colours the way we view all of society.

One of the upshots of moral relativism is that both the adherents of religion and the followers of the "modern myth" are fiercely antagonistic towards evangelical Christians, because they see Christianity as bigoted, claiming a monopoly on truth, intolerant, outdated and hypocritical, whereas they themselves are broad-minded, reasonable, tolerant and loving. The only people they are not tolerant towards are those who oppose them! And this betrays the great contradiction in the philosophy of moral relativism - its adherents believe that relativistic values must hold absolute sway. They have one absolute value, which is that they believe there are no absolutes!

7. Linked to moral relativism is the subject of ethics. Whereas Christianity derives its ethics from the "absolute" moral law and the clear, straightforward teachings of Jesus, religion and the modern myth alike prefer "situational ethics", where the rules of conduct are not fixed but are dependent upon the circumstances or "situation". (The euthanasia and abortion debates both hinge on the issue of situational ethics).

8. Christianity stresses the importance of an inward change and inward reality. Religion puts the emphasis on outward ceremony and ritual, with a frequent use of symbols and "sensory stimulus" - beautiful, evocative or mysterious sights, smells and sounds .

9. Christianity makes no appeal to what the Bible calls "the flesh". (We will have cause to examine this term in more detail later.) Jesus' command to his followers was "Deny yourself, take up your cross daily, and follow me". Paul said "Make no provision for the flesh" ... "the flesh lusts against the Spirit, and the Spirit against the flesh" ... "they that are in the flesh cannot please God" (Rom 13:14;

Gal 5:17; Rom 8:8). Religion, by contrast, often appeals strongly to the flesh, in much the same way as art and music do in themselves. It feels good, beautiful, and comforting. The message of Christianity, by contrast, is not at first comforting but exposing, convicting and humbling. In brief, Christianity deals immediately and ruthlessly with the flesh, whereas religion tends to pander to it.

10. For a Christian, reality comes from knowing God, from the inner reality of Christ living in us. That is "Christian experience". Our expression of this experience and this reality can take the form of art - music, painting, sculpture, poetry, dance and so on. For Christians, art is *an expression of who we are inwardly*. To put it another way, in Christian values, art reflects life. For religious people it is generally the opposite. The "religious experience" comes from an outside stimulus, whether it be aesthetic in nature (inspired by something beautiful), or induced by meditational rituals which bring about altered states of consciousness; whichever way, the experience always comes from some "thing" outside. This means that religion is chiefly concerned with impression, not expression. If the stimulus or inspiration for "religious experience" is aesthetic, it is actually art that produces the effect. Art, to the religious person, is therefore basically an "impressive" thing; life-changing experiences, values, and a sense of reality, are all gained from art itself. So for the religious person, *life reflects art*.

The media would delight to hear that conclusion, because it coincides exactly with their aim. If the media are a popular extension of the arts, then their aim is for everybody's life to reflect their "art", their image, their myth, and their values. There has always been a debate amongst the artistic community as to whether art reflects life, or life reflects art. If life reflects art, then art is the vital thing, the spring, the spiritual source. But if art reflects life, then life is the vital thing, and art should only be a secondary reflection.

If life reflects art, music ought to be more important to us as Christians than our own life and our Christianity. Music would then in fact become a vital means of enhancing and developing our Christianity, and our experience would be merely a reflection of what we have gained through the inspiration and influence of music and art. But if art reflects life, then our own life and our Christianity should be far more important than music. If music is only an expression and a reflection of our life, the thing that matters above all is the quality of that life and our relationship with God. Everything else depends upon that. Music is not primarily a means of inspiration or a road to spiritual experience, but an expression and reflection of our life and experience.

The Infiltration Of The Myth

Having said that the values of religion/myth and the values of Christianity are completely opposed, this does not mean that Christianity is immune to the possibility of infiltration by the values of myth and religion: quite the contrary, for the values of myth and religion are clearly visible in many areas of the Church today. Since New Testament times, the myths of religion have pressed in upon genuine Christianity, and today we have a strange hybrid, a "speckled bird" displaying an uneasy mix of Christianity and religion. The values of the myth have become the values of our culture, and a good deal of the music we listen to is steeped in the values of that culture. Just as Christianity is always threatened by religion, with its attendant myth and value system, so the music we produce as Christians is always in danger of being permeated by the world's culture, myth, and values.

Christianity And Culture

The Christian music scene is already strong, and developing all the time. But as it has developed, it has grown more and more like the culture it is supposed to run "counter" to. Look, for instance, at the promotional magazines of Christian record companies (which often consist chiefly of reviews of their artists' new albums - favourable reviews, naturally!) and you see exactly the same hype, salesmanship techniques and concern with image as you see in the world. The principles are identical. Moreover, increasingly clamorous voices in church leadership are pressing for Christians to get actively involved in culture; introduce them to the classics, or get into rock, or rap, or mime, or any other art form, as a means of infiltrating and influencing society and culture with Christianity. (It is actually far more effectively accomplishing the opposite - influencing Christianity with the world's culture.)

Once Christians are involved in culture, then the styles and art forms of that culture can be used as a hook to win non-Christians to the gospel - or so the idea goes. But what gospel are they being won to? The gospel of culture! A "gospel" that runs on exactly the same principles and ethos as the world. A "gospel" that embraces hype, salesmanship, image, and all the values that go along with it!

Wherever I go, I see Christians who are heavily into musical culture - pop, classical, or any number of smaller "subcultures". They've been sold the image, and become hooked on it, probably without even realising it. They're culture addicts, and their attitude to music is often no different from that of non-Christian music fans.

What seems on the surface to be part of a "Christian counter-culture" actually turns out to share exactly the same principles as myth and religion. Music appeals to the religious mind; in fact, as we have noted, it often gives people what they like to call a "religious experience" or "spiritual experience". Even within mainstream Christianity, there are many people for whom the greatest "spiritual experiences" are gained from being in the most aesthetically satisfying situations. For some, it is the compelling beauty of the architecture of ancient cathedrals, the quiet atmosphere, the smell of incense, the beautiful robes of the ministers, the sounds of choirboys' pure voices floating into the vast spaces. But all these things, which contribute to the attractiveness (what people like to call the "magic") of ritual and ceremony, are fundamentals of myth, fundamentals of religion, and fundamentals of culture - and they are all opposed to real Christianity, its purpose, and its values.

Moral Relativism At Work

The modern trend towards moral relativism is something that has deeply influenced our whole culture. If we as Christian musicians are not alert to this, we will gradually find ourselves being absorbed into that culture and taking on its values without realising it. The 20th century mythology bases its moral perspective on the idea that nothing is "black and white" or clear-cut; there are no absolute standards. Because of this stance, anyone who claims to know or possess "the truth" is at once labelled as bigoted, short-sighted, fundamentalist, narrow-minded, outdated and hypocritical. Moral relativism holds absolute sway; personal morality (choosing your own morality) is in, absolute truth is out - in fact, it is anathema. The myth tells us that the human condition is not clear-cut, but that man is a complex, grey, ill-defined mixture of good and evil. These values can be clearly seen in the pop music culture. It is now acceptable for a rock band to "do good" by playing for a charitable cause, even to instigate new charities (Band Aid, Live Aid) - just as long as they don't claim to have a monopoly on truth, or claim to have the answers. In fact, it's "in" to admit that you're confused and mixed up, and don't have any answers. If you're "sorted out", you're not acceptable. But if you're grey, you're OK.

The recording industry is, not surprisingly, run according to the same values. Nothing outspoken or absolute in terms of truth is allowed. Even musicians at the top of the culture have pointed this out. The eccentric intellectual rock star Frank Zappa once said that any singer who wants to make a clear-cut statement in his songs is fighting against the odds. "He's got a large filtration system waiting for him right after he finishes his lyrics. First of all there's the A & R [Artists and Recording Department] at the record company that's gonna suggest that he'll never get that song played on the radio. Then there's the record company boss who says that if this guy keeps writing stuff like that he's gonna lose his contract. If for some reason he actually records that song and gets it shipped out, every radio station will refuse to play it. Then of course there's all the press that'll review it negatively because it isn't a nice little dance record. So people are persuaded not to do things like that. Finding a way to get material like that to an audience really is the hard part".[2]

This is typical of the way that the culture dictates its values to people, and, in the name of individual freedom, actually exercises a totalitarian-type stranglehold of censorship over anything that opposes the system's values. Only what conforms to the values of the myth is encouraged.

Death Of A Christian Band

A classic example of a Christian group being absorbed into the world's value system is the Irish rock group U2, currently rated amongst the top bands in the world. U2 started life as a Christian band with an explicitly Christian message, straight, truthful and "tell it like it is". But the bigger they got, the greyer the message became. The values of relativism slowly crept in to their lyrics, and the clear-cut message of the gospel was diluted to "I've still not found what I'm looking for" - a classic relativist's statement of admission that he's "not sure". The band's message changed from a personal challenge to Christianity into a global cry for social justice. But even this move was not enough to satisfy the demands of the media and the culture gurus. Accordingly, after a period of "adjustment", U2 reappeared with a radical change of image, converted wholesale to the new mythology and its values. The media were delighted. Lead singer Bono dressed up as the devil on stage. He had, in the words of one pop journalist, "ridden the wheel of delinquency from church-goer to devil-worshipper". At last, this reviewer noted triumphantly, U2 had come off their high horse and become a self-confessed "supermarket commodity", with Bono a self-styled "rock jerk". At last he had seen the light and "jettisoned his bleeding heart, opting instead for adventures in juvenilia".[3]

This is pure media-speak, the very essence of the values of the culture. Compassion and truth are despised and treated with sarcasm; the values of materialism, trivialism and existentialism are elevated to new heights. Now that the band had been "converted", the media felt free to say what they really thought of the old U2: "They had become pompous and dull, too sure of their own right-on opinions to be engaging, too fond of the sound of their own views and too prone to taking themselves seriously".[4]

To take yourself seriously is a big sin in the values of the new mythology, in the kingdom of relativism, image and myth. "Whatever rock 'n' roll is", confessed Bono, "it's to do with myths, mystery and mischief". Well, there's a confession. Malcolm McLaren, manager of the Sex Pistols, said rock was about "sex, subversion and style". It all amounts to the same thing.

The Ancient Root Of The Modern Myth

U2 are just one example of the pull of culture on musicians who started out telling the gospel. Musical culture is just one part of a giant network of systems throughout western civilization, all designed to conform us to the values of the modern myth, the myth based on the fantasy of image, sold to us through the power of the media. Once it is seen clearly, it is revealed to be a complex and brilliant modernization of "the old lie", the deceit of the serpent in the garden of Eden: "You shall be as gods, knowing good and evil" (Gen 3:5). The myths of the New Age add their voices to persuade us that we are indeed gods, and that each of us can decide our own moral values, our own "good and evil", instead of following what God says. As a result of this, man, who was originally made in the image of God, now takes it upon himself to reverse the situation: God is re made in the image of man. We make God what we want him to be. When we see this ancient root of the modern myth, we can understand why image has become such a major force in society today, in the kingdom of the prince of this world. It plays an essential role in determining the way we think and behave, and sets the standards for our whole ethos and value system. Thought, worldview, behaviour, ethos, values - that is where the devil wants the control.

There is a vital need for Christians today to thoroughly understand about image, its values, and the way it works through the media and culture. Without that understanding we will not escape being pulled in and pulled along by the culture, and we will unconsciously absorb its values and become a part of the system we are supposed to challenge and oppose. But if we become aware of what is going on, we can spot the dangers as they begin to show up in "Christian culture", and react with a true counter-culture - one that runs on opposite principles to the world. This is a real and exciting possibility, which we shall be exploring in Part III. But to conclude our overview of trends in the church and in society, we need to consider an issue which lies at the heart of everything we have been discussing: freedom of choice.

Notes

1. Alvin Toffler, *Future Shock* (Pan Books, 1971), p 147
2. Frank Zappa, speaking at a press conference in 1988, quoted by Tony Bacon in *Making Music*, Feb 1994.
3. *The Sunday Times Magazine*, 25th July 1993
4. *ibid.*

Chapter 21

Choice

When people are free to do as they please, they generally imitate each other.

Eric Hoffer

Choice is at the centre of Christianity. Free will is an essential Christian doctrine, standing in stark opposition to the claims of Hinduism and Buddhism that we are born with a burden of *karma*, the result of actions in our "previous lives" which control our present condition and future destiny. Free will and choice also run contrary to the fatalistic, occult viewpoint of astrology, which states that the circumstances of our lives and the nature of our characters are predetermined and fixed. The widespread acceptance of such a view is demonstrated by the continuing popularity of horoscopes.

The issues of image, myth, and cultural values which we have been considering all beg an important question: How much free choice do we actually have in our 20th century western civilization? Are we really free to choose, or are our choices being made for us?

As members of a democratic society, we tend to take it for granted that we are free agents, able to make personal choices about every aspect of our lives, from the music we listen to and the food we eat to the religions and values we believe in and uphold. But is this really the case? Amongst the myriad sociological interpretations of modern society, there are two opposing schools of thought regarding human choice. The first view is championed by such noted figures as the historian Arnold Toynbee, and Jacques Ellul, a French sociologist and radical Christian thinker, who warns that we are rushing headlong into a totalitarian-type state where everything is standardized and choice is removed. Choice in such a society, states Ellul, is no longer a real possibility. "The human being is no longer in any sense the agent of choice".[1]

The other side of the argument is proposed by Alvin Toffler, who ridicules Ellul's "technophobia", pointing out that in fact, the opposite is happening - we are actually experiencing a massive de-standardization in every area of society, and being presented with more and more diversity and variety of choice. The problem of the future, maintains Toffler, will not be lack of choice but "overchoice" - a bewildering array of technologies, subcultures and lifestyles to choose from.[2]

In fact, both theories are partly true, but only tell half the story. We are certainly faced today with an extraordinary variety of choice in every area of our lives. To that extent, Toffler is correct. But Ellul rightly perceives that the apparent diversity of choice is only a front, behind which lies an equally astonishing conformity of values right across the board - and these values turn out to be the values of the myth, appearing in a thousand different guises. It is this aspect of conformity which gives rise to Ellul's suspicions about the rise of a "velvet-gloved totalitarian state" exercising a subtle but all-pervading control over the way we think and behave.

The role of the media presents us with the key to the apparent contradiction posed by Toffler's and Ellul's views. For although the mass media are largely responsible for presenting us with so much "overchoice", the same media also provide the main vehicle for the values of the myth, sold to us through image. The apparent diversity of choice which confronts us is a smoke-screen obscuring the fact that our "choice" is no choice at all. Whichever lifestyle, subculture or new technology we choose, we are actually not choosing or thinking for ourselves at all - merely accepting an "off-the-peg" set of values from the bewildering array, all of which turn out to reflect the same ethos and point us in the same anti-christian direction.

Unity In Diversity

What both Toffler and Ellul have overlooked is a concept which has become one of the major slogans of the New Age Movement - "unity in diversity". This phrase was first coined by Alice Bailey, a theosophist and pioneer of the New Age Movement. Steeped in occult practices, Bailey learned the expression "unity in diversity" from her spirit guide, who she called her "Tibetan Master".

Constance Cumbey, a Christian author writing about the New Age, says, "According to New Age sources, the New Age Movement is a world-wide network. It consists of tens of thousands of co-operating organizations. Their primary goal, or the secret behind their 'unity in diversity', is the formation of a 'New World Order'."[3]

The world has since heard that same phrase "New World Order" from the lips of U.S. Presidents Bush and Clinton. That fact alone should give us a fair idea of the influence of the New Age today. Their huge "network" of organizations throughout the political, commercial, technological and arts/ media arenas of the world is not a structured linkage of organizations at all. On the surface they often appear to be quite unrelated - one more manifestation of "overchoice". But they all share the same basic values and contribute in their own way to the same aim. That is "unity in diversity". A New Age author explains: "A network is many times greater than the sum of its parts. This is a source of power never before tapped in history: multiple self-sufficient social movements linked for a whole array of goals whose accomplishment would transform every aspect of contemporary life ... You can't destroy the network by destroying a single leader or some vital organ. The centre - the heart - of the network is everywhere".[4]

There is actually an organization called "The Unity in Diversity Council", which is apparently "a world-wide co-ordinating body of organizations and individuals 'fostering the emergence of a new universal person and civilization based on unity-in-diversity among all peoples' ". Among the events they co-ordinate are "festivals for mind-body-spirit", billed as "an expression of our unity-in-diversity through art, media, entertainment, lectures and workshops, alternative technologies and the experience of oneness".[5]

The Musical Network

The arts and media represent only one segment of the "network"; and music, with its own "overchoice" of musical styles, represents only a small part of that segment. But no matter how diverse they appear on the surface, each style turns out under examination to share the same ethos and value system - that of the New Age religion, which is that of the myth. It is a world-wide movement, bigger than the New Age itself: the New Age is merely the current spearheading movement, acting as one more catalyst in the immense plan to bring about what is prophesied in the book of Revelation - the culmination of the world's system in the kingdom of antichrist.

Who else could have so brilliantly engineered a world-wide control of values and thought systems, but the prince of this world himself? That is the force and scope of what we are up against. But we do not have to fall in line; we do not have to conform to the pattern; indeed, it is essential that we do not. *There is an alternative.*

Notes

1. Jaques Ellul, *The Technological Society*, (Vintage Books, 1967) p.80
2. Toffler, *op. cit.*, p.240
3. Constance Cumbey, *The Hidden Dangers of the Rainbow* (Huntington House, 1983) p.54
4. Marilyn Ferguson, *The Aquarian Conspiracy* (J.P. Tarcher, 1980), p.216
5. Cumbey, *op. cit.*, p.211

Part III

THE CHRISTIAN ALTERNATIVE

The glory of the gospel is that when the Church is absolutely different from the world, she invariably attracts it.

Martyn Lloyd-Jones

God creates things out of nothing.
Therefore until a man is nothing,
God can make nothing out of him.

Martin Luther

Chapter 22

The Christian's Purpose

I sought for a man ...
Ezekiel 22:30

We have spent a long time looking at the "wrong road", the dangers, abuses and misconceptions that, unfortunately, seem to abound in the Christian music sphere. It's time to look at the positive side! There is most certainly a proper use of music, a use which is in line with God's purpose for Christians. There is a way of utilizing music as a vehicle for God's Spirit, and there is a genuine place of power against the devil and his kingdom.

The Purpose Of Music

God has a purpose for music, and a means for achieving that purpose.

The purpose of music is as a means of *expression*. Expression is not just a feature of music; music is primarily and fundamentally a means of expression. It finds its greatest and highest use when a person full of God's Spirit expresses his or her heart, perhaps in worship to God, perhaps in proclamation to others, perhaps in other ways. Music is simply an expressive device, a medium for expressive power, through which a Christian can express the Spirit of God.

The means for achieving this expression of God's Spirit is *people*. That may sound obvious, but it has important implications:

1. God works through *people*, not through *music*. One of the things that is wrong with the "magic formula mentality" discussed in Chapter 16 is that it presupposes that God works directly through "things", of which music can be one example. God never works directly through music. He works directly through people, through their conscious, willing spirits. When they express themselves and play music, His Spirit may be expressed through them; but it is incorrect to say that God is working through the music. God is working through the people who are expressing themselves through music.

2. Similarly, God anoints *people*, not music. His presence comes through people, again, not directly through things. His power works through people, not music. This is a fundamental principle of the way God works, and a key to understanding the role of music and its proper use.

Your Life Is The Key

This means that it is your life, your personal relationship with God, that is the key. I may be very skilful and able to play very beautiful music, and I may use it to minister to God and to others - but I may nevertheless see precious little fruit for my efforts. However, an old man with an out-of-tune guitar may carry God's anointing so powerfully that many lives are changed through him! What makes the difference? *Your life*. It's certainly a good thing to be able to play or sing well. But if you're a Christian musician, you should be preparing yourself more than you prepare the music. Of course practice is important. Of course you should prepare the music as well. But it's your life that is the channel for God. A more holy life, a more surrendered life, a more humbled life will be a better channel for God. But better music will not be a better channel for God. If more beautiful or skilful music was a better channel for God, if music was the key, then we all ought to be practising more. But it is our personal life, not music, that is the key to successful "music ministry" - and any other type of ministry - so our emphasis should be on praying more rather than practising more.

Understanding "Talents".

We commonly use the word "talent" to describe a particular natural gift, skill or ability, whether it be in music, gymnastics or mathematics. We derive this meaning from the word used in the "parable of the talents" (Mt 25:14-30). However, in that parable, a "talent" does not mean a skill or gift at all! It means an amount of money. A talent was a weight of gold or silver, and therefore a unit of money, worth about 6,000 denarii in Jesus' day (many thousands of pounds by today's standards). The parable has been universally interpreted as if it was about our natural skills and abilities, and how we use them. But it is much nearer the mark to say that the "talent" refers to the most precious resource that every Christian has: the Spirit of God, the life of Christ within you, the "measure of faith" which has been given to you (Rom 12:3). This is the "commodity" with which we trade, and, as a result, produce more of the same.

If the "talents" refer only to natural abilities, this principle of "producing more" would be nonsense, as if God wanted us to produce more skill and talent in the world, and our heavenly reward would be based on that. In that case, a great violinist is automatically a great saint! Pity, then, the people who aren't talented! But if the "talents" speak of the life of God within us, then the principle of "producing more" corresponds exactly with Jesus' image of the vine bearing fruit: it is planted as one seed, which came from one fruit; but its purpose is to "bear much fruit".

Spiritual reproduction is one of God's principles. Everything in creation reproduces "after its kind" (Gen 1:11); sheep produce sheep, grapes produce grapes, humans produce humans - and God's life produces more of God's life. If at the end of your life you can say you have been a vehicle for God's Spirit and an expression of His life, to the extent that many others have benefited from that life - then that is a life well spent, deserving of the words "well done, good and faithful servant". Such a person has done God's work, fulfilled God's purpose, and expressed God's life. That is our aim!

So if we understand "talents" to mean the life of Christ within us, it is important for us to strive, not primarily to be better musicians, but to be better ministers of God's life.

Ministry

Christian ministry means, fundamentally, sharing and expressing God's life. We can do that *through* many things; music, words, scriptures, acts of mercy and compassion, and so on. But music in itself is not ministry. It is the life of God that is "ministered" and expressed. We have already noted the difference between expression and impression. Ministry is always an expression of some sort. It may be "ministry to God". Such a term is scriptural (see Acts 13:2 - although in that context it seems to have more to do with prayer and fasting than music - a point worth noting!); or it may be ministry to others. Ministry to God is often termed "worship".

Worship is the expression of an attitude of heart, yielding, surrendered, obedient and willing. Worship is not to do with high praise or soft singing. It is not even to do with the presence of God. Worship is about submission, consecration and sacrifice. The first mention of "worship" in the Bible is from the lips of Abraham: "I and the lad will go yonder and worship" (Gen 22:5). Abraham was not going to have a "chorus time"; he was going to perform the most costly act of surrender of his whole life - an act of literal sacrifice. In laying Isaac on the altar, Abraham was laying everything on the altar. And it is this that Abraham calls "worship".

When music is a vehicle for obedient, submissive, consecrated Christians to express themselves, great things can happen. The expressive force of music is such that it releases, carries and transmits what is in the "expresser's" spirit with tremendous effectiveness, often far more powerfully than words alone. There can indeed be a release of God's Spirit through music. But we must understand that the release is through people, and only indirectly "through music" because of them. Everything depends on the quality of the people, not the quality of the music.

The Anointing

There can certainly be times when we feel a tremendous sense of God's presence (which is often called "the anointing") when we are using music in worship. But once again we must remember that it is people, not music, that carry this anointing. Surprisingly, considering the amount of teaching that goes around on the subject, the only place in the entire New Testament where the phrase "the anointing" occurs is 1 Jn 2:27: "The anointing which you have received from him abides in you". This clearly implies that the anointing is something that all Christians have in some measure (like the talents), and that (as with all the manifestations of God's life) the key to its release lies in the quality of our relationship with God, and our expression of that relationship.

With this brief overview of basic concepts in mind, we can now go on to look at the subject of music ministry in more detail.

Chapter 23

The Key To Ministry: Brokenness

The fact is, we have too much strength. We are not weak enough. It is not our strength that we want. One drop of God's strength is worth more than all the world.

D. L. Moody

How do we release the life of God, the "anointing which we have received", which "abides in us"? Firstly, we need to recognise that there is something which naturally tends to stop the life of God from flowing out of us - the flesh. The word "flesh" needs some explanation. In the Bible it covers a broad spectrum of meaning. It can mean "the physical substance of the body" (as in "flesh and blood"), or "mankind" (as in "All flesh is grass" or "I will pour out My Spirit upon all flesh"). But in the vast majority of references in the New Testament, it clearly means the corrupt, Adamic element in our nature. The characteristics of "the flesh" are opposition to God (Rom 8:7, Gal 5:17), independence and self-reliance (Phil 3:3-4, Jn 8:15), arrogance, pride, boastfulness, and self-exaltation (2 Cor 11:18, 1 Cor 1:29), corruption and unprofitability (Gal 6:8, Jn 6:63), and concern with image and reputation (Gal 6:12-13). Paul says that the "mind set on the flesh is death" (Rom 8:6); Jeremiah declares, "Cursed is the man who makes flesh his arm", (Jer 17:5) and Paul affirms that "those who are Christ's have crucified the flesh" (Gal 5:24). It is worth studying these scriptures for yourself, in order to become familiarized with the biblical picture.

Break Me, Melt Me , Mould Me

This flesh, this proud, independent self-life, has to be broken, if we are to be able to minister God's life. The theme song of the charismatic movement used to be, "Spirit of the living God, fall afresh on me ... break me, melt me, mould me, fill me..." This chorus seems to have all but disappeared today, perhaps because of over-use in the past. But it has not been replaced by anything else which speaks of the desire for brokenness. In fact, some years ago it was rather tellingly superseded by a similar chorus which shares an identical first line, but the words "break me, melt me, mould me" are replaced by the repeated phrase "fill me anew". Is this symptomatic of the way our thinking is going? Do we want to be filled without having to be broken? Are we only interested in being filled, and not with being melted, moulded and used? Whatever the case, there seems to be no doubt about the scriptural principle: for the life of God to flow out from us to others, there needs to be a brokenness, a death, inside us - death to self and the flesh, a death to self-will and our own way, a yielding up to God of every area of that independent, self-assertive flesh life which constantly opposes God's way.

Paul says, "the flesh lusts against the Spirit, and the Spirit against the flesh" (Gal 5:17). And in 2 Corinthians 4, where Paul is talking specifically about ministry (v.1) he makes reference to the treasure (the life of God) which we have "in earthen vessels" (v.7), and again makes the principle clear: "...always bearing about in the body the dying of the Lord Jesus, that the life also of Jesus might be made manifest in our body. For we which live are always delivered unto death for Jesus' sake, that the life also of Jesus might be made manifest in our mortal flesh. So then death works in us, but life in you" (2 Cor 4:10-12).

In Paul, death was working - his flesh was constantly

being broken - but because of this brokenness, the life of God within him was always flowing out to others. He was always bearing fruit. Life, God's life, was working in them, because of death working in him.

The Precious Ointment

We see the same principle in the incident recorded in Matthew's gospel (Mt 26:6-13) where a woman took a jar of very costly ointment, broke the jar, and poured the ointment over Jesus' head. This is a perfect illustration of what brokenness means. We have a costly treasure - the anointing, the life of God - in us, just as the ointment was in the jar; but as the ointment was sealed inside the jar, so that none of the fragrance could escape without the jar first being broken, so God's life is "sealed" inside our flesh, and unless that flesh is broken, the "anointing", the life of Jesus, will not be able to get out. As long as this is the case, we will actually have no true ministry at all, no matter how talented, experienced, dedicated or hard-working we may be: no matter if we prepare meticulously and pray ever so hard; unless there is brokenness, there will be no life of God, no results of eternal value, no real ministry.

Breaking The Jar

The ointment was in an alabaster jar. This is quite significant. Alabaster was not a cheap material by any means; the jar was costly in itself. But it was as nothing compared to the value of the ointment. We can see in this a picture of our natural talents, skills and abilities. They are, of course, "God-given" in the sense that everything we have and are is God-given; and natural gifts and talents have a value. They are not "cheap", and certainly not worthless. Like the alabaster jar, they are carefully crafted out of fine material. But the jar had to be broken, and our natural strengths have to be broken, no matter how valuable they may seem to us. We have to yield ourselves to God; we have to lay down our talents before Him - and then it is God who has to take us and break us. We cannot effect this brokenness ourselves. We can only do two things: firstly, realise our need of brokenness; secondly, put ourselves in the position where God can bring it about in us.

When God does the work of brokenness (and He knows exactly how to do it in each of our lives, through our circumstances, relationships, trials, sometimes even through tragedy), then the miracle happens - the precious ointment is released. The Spirit of God is released to minister through us. The life of Jesus is "made manifest in our mortal flesh", and flows out to others. John's version of the story records that "the whole house was filled with the fragrance of the ointment", or, if you like, "with the anointing" (Jn 12:3). This is true ministry, to God and to men, where the fragrance of Christ is manifested and spread around. This is true fruit-bearing, where God's life "reproduces after its kind". We are then "a sweet fragrance of Christ" to God and to others.

Treasure In Earthen Vessels

Notwithstanding the value of our natural gifts and skills, Paul says that "we have this treasure in earthen vessels" - jars of clay. We have seen that natural talent does not make a better vehicle for the life of God or for true ministry. In fact, the scriptural weight is on the side of the opposite argument - that natural skills and strength can tend to obstruct the life of God, and that for this reason "God has chosen the foolish things of the world ... the weak things ... the base things ... the things which are despised" (1 Cor 1:27-28).

The reason why God has done things this way is found in the next verse (the key to the whole chapter): "that no flesh should glory in His presence" (1 Cor 1:29). This means that the flesh has to go. If the flesh is present, it will always glory in what it can do - in its natural talents, strengths, abilities, and gifts. So many of the basic driving forces that propel us through life must now be dealt with: ambition, ego, self-interest, independence, reputation. God will not use unbroken talent, because there is flesh in it. God's anointing and flesh cannot dwell together. "The anointing oil ... shall not be poured upon man's flesh" (Ex 30:32). Flesh and God's glory cannot dwell together (1 Cor 1:29). Flesh and God's Spirit cannot dwell together (Gal 5:17). However, there are many Christians who sincerely believe that they are ministering for God, when in fact they are spending their lives fulfilling their natural ambition on God's stage. The products of such "ministry" are at best shallow, and at worst counterfeit. People may get blessed, people may even get saved under their ministry. But that doesn't mean that the ministry is happening the way God intends. It only means that God is compassionate and merciful, and that He will use any situation and any vessel He can.

The Body and The Flesh

One of the more disturbing trends in charismatic worship today is a growing ignorance of what the Bible means by "the flesh", and a confusion between the flesh and the body. One recent book on worship surprisingly displays this ignorance by quoting approvingly an instance where a church member had criticized the church's worship as being "fleshly". "Absolutely right" was the worship leader's reply. "I do not have an out of the body experience when I worship God."[1] One review of the book commented favourably on this statement, saying that "worship was never meant to be cerebral" but "involves our whole being".[2] Whilst it is quite reasonable to suggest that worship should have physical elements, the implicit equation of "physical" and "fleshly" is quite amazing - for it seems plain that the quoted critic of the worship was not finding fault with the physical aspects of the worship but with the fact that he/she found it "fleshly". It is astonishing that the author of the book, and its reviewer, should appear to have no conception of what the Bible means by "the flesh".

If we confuse "physical" with "fleshly", we are actually well on the way to heresy. For as we have seen, the Bible says many times that the flesh is bad; and if we equate the flesh with the physical body, we end up saying that the body is evil, and creating an opposition between spiritual and physical things (spiritual things are good, physical things are evil). This is, of course, utterly anti-scriptural. The Bible never says that the body is evil. Perhaps it was to combat this error that the quoted worship leader made his remarks. But they have fallen into equal error on the other side, because they fail to distinguish between the body and the flesh, and therefore run the danger of accepting behaviour and attitudes that the Bible denounces as anti-God and incompatible with God.

The Root Of The Problem

This confusion is not an isolated incident or an unrepresentative view, but part of a much broader trend, which has its roots in the reaction of the "charismatic generation" to the previous generation - the early 20th century evangelicals and pentecostals. This earlier generation, as we have seen in Chapter 13, contained an element which tended to call anything that did not come within their strict moral confines "worldly" or "fleshly". Cinema, "dance halls" and television (known in the early days as the "hellevision!") are a few well-known examples. The following generation of Christians reacted against what they perceived as shallow, legalistic prudery; and the terms "worldly", "fleshly" and "natural" have since become the subject of gentle mockery in the hands of Christian humorists like Adrian Plass. Although it is no bad thing to expose hypocrisy, legalism and bigotry, there has unfortunately been a subtle subversion running along with this trend. The casting-off of outmoded terms ("worldliness", "fleshly") which were seen to be related to legalistic, prudish attitudes, has also resulted in the casting-off of the biblical concepts of "the flesh" and "the world". The very terms have now become virtually synonymous with out-dated "Victorian" scruples. Moreover, while the words have gone out of fashion, no equivalent terms have come in to replace them. This can mean only one thing: that the Church is losing the concept of what "the flesh" means.

Losing The Distinction

Christians' attitudes to "the world" are usually paralleled by their attitudes to "the flesh"; and it seems that both concepts are slowly disappearing. The distinction between "the spirit" and "the flesh" is no longer a meaningful one to many Christians. Is that because we are not sure we can tell the difference any more? In a day when "worship" has come to mean music, often performed to very high standards, utilizing amazing technology which puts stunning, captivating sounds within the reach of anyone who wants to call themselves a musician - are we losing a fundamental intuitive distinction which lies at the roots of Christianity? Are we in danger of becoming blind to the difference between the flesh and the spirit? Does "the flesh" only convey to us the idea of over-indulgence in food or sex? Are we no different from the world, to whom "the sins of the flesh" simply mean adultery or fornication?

At this point in time, as I see it, many churches are in a dangerous place. If the sense of distinction between flesh and spirit becomes virtually eliminated, and we fail to discern between what is of purely natural, human origin in our "worship" and what is of God, we can too easily become convinced that our meetings are attended by God's anointing (when in reality they are attended by manipulative, evocative forces acting through very well performed music, coupled with the corporate atmosphere which naturally descends on a group of people who share the same basic unity of purpose). We are then primed for increasingly fundamental errors to creep in. The ministers of Satan, disguised as ministers of righteousness (2 Cor 11:15) are ready-armed with false anointing, deceptive signs and wonders, and "lies in truth's clothing", patiently waiting for their moment to strike, subtle and unnoticed, at the heart of Christianity.

Is this just alarmist scaremongering? I hope that's all it proves to be. I don't want it to happen; but the problem is that I see it happening already. In Chapter 15 we have seen one example. The trend is now here.

The Christian's Attitude Towards The Flesh

We need to react with the opposite trend. If we are involved in "music ministry", then we need, as ministers, to have crucified the flesh (Gal 5:24). When Paul went to Corinth with the message of the gospel, he was quite adequately trained as a speaker, he knew the scriptures thoroughly, and he could easily have relied on his natural ability. Immediately after his conversion he had preached in the synagogues at Damascus, "confounding the Jews ... proving that Jesus is the true Christ" (Acts 9:22). But by the time he visited Corinth, many years later, Paul had learned a lesson about the flesh. So, by his own testimony, he did not come "with excellence of speech or of wisdom", even though he could have done so; but "I determined not to know anything among you, save Jesus Christ, and him crucified.

And I was with you in weakness, and in fear, and in much trembling". This is the sign of a man whose flesh has been dealt with. "And my speech and my preaching was not with enticing words of man's wisdom, but in demonstration of the Spirit and of power: that your faith should not stand in the wisdom of men, but in the power of God" (1 Cor 2:1-5).

Man's Insufficiency, God's Strength

So it must be with us. If people are going to be converted to faith in God, not to faith in music or culture, or to a false Christianity based on human strength and wisdom, then we must present to them Christ crucified, the wisdom and power of God. To do that, we need, like Paul, to lay aside our natural strengths and abilities, and learn to be weak, fearful and trembling! Often we misunderstand when there is talk of weakness and fear. Christians protest that they have been delivered from such things. But we may be suffering from a basic misconception. We all willingly admit that we are entirely dependent on God for our salvation. But we are not so willing to remain dependent upon Him thereafter, and we soon return to our own strength, re-arming ourselves with self-confidence, self-reliance and self-sufficiency, the very attitudes that we at first laid down at the foot of the cross. It is this change of principles that Paul referred to when he remonstrated with the Galatians: "Having begun in the Spirit, are you now made perfect by the flesh?" (Gal 3:3). We must remain dependent on God, always conscious of our own insufficiency. That's how God's power is best displayed, and that's how God's life is best ministered - when we are reliant upon Him, knowing we can do nothing of ourselves. Only this knowledge will drive us to meaningful prayer, fasting, and all those attitudes which characterize the person whose flesh has been dealt with (described perfectly by Jesus in the Sermon on the Mount, Matthew chapters 5, 6 and 7 - see especially Mt 5:1-6, 6:1-18).

Notes

1. Noel Richards, *The Worshipping Church* (Pioneer Perspectives, 1993) p.35
2. Henry Drabble, in *Redemption Magazine*, Jan 1994

Chapter 24

Ministry To Others

Is not this the fast that I have chosen? to loose the bands of wickedness, to undo the heavy burdens, and to let the oppressed go free, and that you break every yoke?

Isaiah 58:6

So far we have discussed corporate and personal worship, areas where everyone is an active participant. Clearly the purpose of music here is to provide a vehicle for people's expression. Ministry to others, however, is different, because it involves the situation of "performer and audience", if I can put it in those terms: the performer singing or playing (expression) and the audience on the receiving end (being "impressed").

In Chapter 5 we noted some of the negative aspects of impression, and classed them as an abuse of music's powers. Expression, of course, is not the only legitimate use of music; it can't be! Every expression has someone else on the receiving end of it, being "impressed". Any performance, whether it is live or recorded, is designed to be listened to - designed, that is, for impression. The whole point of using music as "ministry to others" is that others are beneficially "impressed" or influenced by the music.

It is also true that no-one can express anything unless they have first been impressed themselves. *Nothing can come out of us that hasn't first gone in to us.* This is because only God is truly original. Only God can create, in the pure sense of that word. No-one else can, neither humans, nor angels, nor the devil. As Christians, we can express, but we can never create, in the absolute sense of the term. Moreover, we can never express anything genuinely original, for we can only express what we have first been impressed by. "There is nothing new under the sun", as Solomon said; and Paul's rhetorical question "What do you have that you have not received?" (1 Cor 4:7) is true of everything about us.

Outside Influence

We are vessels for God's Spirit, and temples of the Holy Spirit. What we may call "Christian impression" or inspiration comes from God, the indweller of that temple. Before we become Christians, the "impression" comes from outside ourselves, when God is drawing us to Himself, but once His Spirit comes to dwell in us, impression comes from within. As we have seen, John tells us that the anointing (which we may be used to thinking of as a "presence" or atmosphere that comes from "outside") is, scripturally, *within us*: it "abides in you" (1 Jn 2:27). Christian inspiration and impression, therefore, come from within. So our expression and impression both have the same source - the Spirit of God within us.

Impression as such, "the receiving end of expression", is entirely legitimate. It obviously can't be a bad thing in itself, otherwise we could not be impressed by God's Spirit, either through music, or words, or visions in our mind. Nevertheless, it is worth recognising that all these "vehicles for God's Spirit" are open to a similar sort of abuse: visions become dangerous when they become deliberate visualisation; words become dangerous when they become slogans and tools for brainwashing; and music becomes dangerous when we deliberately set out to use it as a stimulant in order to change the way we feel, or to bring about a "presence" or atmosphere. Used in this way it can so easily become a substitute for God, an excuse for not dealing with reality, a doorway into fantasy, idolatry and introspection.

However, the desire to be influenced by God, or to influence others, is not wrong at all. In fact, without it there would be no gospel - for the gospel itself is, in a sense, an influence or impression (others receiving the expression of the good news). Moreover, without impression there would be no ministry to others. There are counterfeits, there are substitutes, and impression is an area fraught with danger if we do not understand it properly. But a person filled with God, carrying and expressing God's Spirit, communicating and overflowing to others - that's the real thing, and we need to receive and be impressed by that!

How we handle impression - the influences we come under or subject ourselves to in our own lives - is an important issue that calls for wisdom and discernment. Each one of us needs to learn, by regular prayer and communication with God, to recognize the difference between the Spirit of God and the often very subtle counterfeits and substitutes that creep in. But there are of course many times when we can legitimately receive, or be impressed by, music - when it is a true vehicle for God's Spirit - and there are times when we can all benefit from that sort of ministry.

David And Saul

The classic scriptural example of music used in ministry is found in 1 Samuel 16. David played the harp for the oppressed King Saul, and as a result, an evil spirit departed from Saul (1 Sam 16:23). This incident is regarded as one of the scriptural foundations for the concept of "music ministry" - and I think rightly so, although there are a few things to note about it:

1. The evil spirit did not depart from Saul *for ever* - it always came back.

2. The evil spirit did not *always* depart - once, even as David was playing, the evil spirit came upon Saul, and he threw a javelin at David. (1 Sam 18:10-11)

3. The evil spirit was sent *from God* (1 Sam 16:14,23; 18:10) because the Spirit of God had left Saul as a result of his disobedience. David's music could do nothing to cure that disobedience.

4. In the end, the music ministry did not succeed in anything more than a temporary alleviation of Saul's problem. The problem was deeper than any music or deliverance ministry could deal with; it was a problem of disobedience and self-will. Only repentance and humility can solve that sort of problem.

5. Although we have said that brokenness is the key to ministry and to the release of the anointing, it should not be inferred that this constitutes a foolproof path to power. There are no "magic formulas" for God's presence and power. This is an important lesson for us. David's ministry succeeded one day and failed the next, even though his heart attitude was always right. We cannot predict or guarantee results with God. He is sovereign.

However, we can say that when Saul was troubled, the ministry of David was, at least temporarily, effective. There are again a couple of points worth noting here:

1. The key lay in David, not the music. The Spirit of the Lord was upon David (1 Sam 16:13). The anointing "remained in him". The anointing was not in the music; the music was only the vehicle for the expression of an anointed man.

2. David was not the "court minstrel". He was not an entertainer. He was brought in specifically to minister to a troubled soul (1 Sam 16:15-19).

Ministry Is For Troubled Souls

The message for us here is this: *music can really minister to troubled souls*. David was expressing himself; Saul was at the "impression" end of it. To be on the receiving end of music, to be using it as "impression", is perfectly alright. If you are troubled in spirit, music can genuinely minister to you. But it is designed to minister to troubled, broken, humbled spirits - *not to egos*; that is, not to people who have no needs except the need to be entertained. As musicians, we should ensure that we are ministering to those who need ministry - to needs, not to egos.

Speaking personally, I have found that it is when I am ministering in prisons or Young Offenders Institutes that I am most conscious of doing a worthwhile job. When I am ministering to people who I know are troubled, I am the most satisfied in my own heart that the music is doing a real work. My greatest encouragements have come from prisoners; their comments have shown me that they understand what I am trying to do, and that it does have a real effect. They realise that I don't just want to entertain them and take their minds off their problems for an hour. They know they need a more radical solution than that. They know they are troubled souls; no-one makes trouble outside unless they are troubled inside. And *God wants to minister to troubled souls.*

Ministry to egos is just entertainment. The spirit of entertainment is catching on in church. It has nothing whatsoever to do with ministry in the true sense of the word. All it ministers to is people's egos - it builds up the flesh, and satisfies self. That, of course, is the reason why anybody goes to a concert, or for a night out. The satisfaction of self is not what Christianity is about - yet it is becoming an increasingly prominent aspect of church meetings. We are in danger of becoming a spiritually decadent people, forever seeking blessing, alarmingly similar to those whom Amos denounced for being "at ease in Zion" (Amos 6:1) "... that lie upon beds of ivory, and stretch themselves upon their couches, and eat the lambs out of the flock ... that chant to the sound of the viol, and invent to themselves instruments of music like David; that drink wine in bowls, and anoint themselves with the best ointments: but they are not grieved for the affliction of Joseph" (Amos 6:4-6).

A World Of Luxury

Amos' prophecy recognizes the importance of music in a decadent culture. Notice that is not the music, but the way it is used, that is wrong; it is the people's attitude that is at fault and needs correction. For David himself, as the prophecy said, made "instruments of music", and ordained Levitical worship in the tabernacle; but David knew that relationship with God comes first and foremost; music is nothing compared to that. However, to the people in Amos' day, music was more important. They had become a society hooked on self-satisfaction - on wine, food, luxury and entertainment.

This is a fair description of society today. Our world, in the prosperous western nations, is one of luxury. Luxury is our contemporary lifestyle, whether in relation to food, clothes, cars, houses, work, wages or recreation. But that is no surprise. The surprise, and the shame, is that it is also a description of *Christian* society. It is all a far cry from the biblical injunction: "Having [enough] food and clothes, let us be content" (1 Tim 6:8); or Jesus' command: "Lay not up for yourselves treasures on earth ... take no thought for your life, what you shall eat ... nor for your body, what you shall put on ... is not the life [spiritual life] more than food? ... But seek first the Kingdom of God, and His righteousness" (Mt 6:19,25,33).

We must be alert to the role of music in such a society, and to the abuses of music which result from society's attitudes. We must be even more alert to the danger of the spirit of the world infiltrating the church, in the form of entertainment, and the crucial role music plays in that. We must never allow ourselves to become a part of such proceedings. If we do, we will set a precedent in our own lives which we will find hard to break afterwards, and we will be guilty of encouraging the church in the wrong direction. If we have a share in leading congregations, we are ministers, and we share in the shepherd's responsibility; so we will also be judged as the shepherds and teachers are judged. (Read Jas 3:1 and Ezk 34:1-31 to get a sober and accurate view of what this responsibility involves).

Expressing Yourself

It may seem a digression from the subject of music to be talking about personal lifestyle. But I know that the answers to the proper use of music, the purpose for which God intended it, and effective ministry, lie not in examining music, but in examining ourselves, which means examining the way we live. Our lifestyle and behaviour are the only accurate reflections of our Christianity. Our words mean nothing by themselves. Talk is cheap! It's how we live before God that counts, and that determines whether we are of use to Him.

We have said that the expression of our own spirit is a key to ministry. That necessarily implies certain constraints upon our music-making. We need, for instance, to down-play the role and influence of the other powers which music can convey, recognize what those powers involve, and we must ensure that we make them entirely subservient to our own spirit's expression. The music must say what we want to say; it must be a vehicle for the expression of what is within us. If we start getting inspired by the music, that's the wrong way round. It is our part to express, not to be impressed.

In the Christian use of music, the hierarchy of importance is as follows: 1) GOD'S SPIRIT; 2) YOUR SPIRIT; 3) THE WORDS; 4) THE MUSIC.

The music comes lowest of all. *The music must serve and support the words*, not take over them, nor be more beautiful, captivating or powerful than them. Otherwise people get distracted from the words and onto the music. Next, *the words must serve, suit and support you*, your spirit, your expression of those words. If you cannot truly put your spirit into those words and mean them from your heart, you are not ministering. And finally, most importantly, *you must serve and support God*, and your spirit must be an expression of His Spirit. This of course demands a living, healthy relationship with God, nurtured by a consistent prayer life.

So the music is a vehicle for the words; the words are a vehicle for you; and you are a vehicle for God. Once you have chosen or written words that express what you want to say, or what God wants to say, and you have set them to music (which, when fully arranged, is not going to overpower the words, either in volume or in emotional force), then you have to ensure that other powers working through the music are not going to overpower your spirit.

Charismatic Personalities

One of the marks of great singers and musicians in the world is their force of personality. To be skilful or to have a great voice is not enough. You have to captivate the audience and carry them along with you. What the world calls the "charismatic personality" of a performer is the decisive factor in their influence and effect. We understand this "charisma" to be, simply, the force of human spirit. Great artists seem to be able to fill a hall or a theatre with their presence, and this is purely the result of their expression of their own spirit. They carry their own "anointing", if I may put it that way without irreverence. Now we are intended to carry God's anointing. We are meant to be the tabernacles of God (1 Cor 3:16, 6:19). When I hear a recording of a Christian singer that really ministers to me, it is always because they have struck the right balance; the music is not more interesting, compelling or powerful than the words; the words carry conviction and spirit because of the singer's expressive capability; the singer's spirit comes across as the dominant force; and the whole thing is saying something, which speaks as from God's Spirit.

But it is unusual to find this balance. Lyrics are often shallow and trite, unrelated to practical experience, and in the end, saying nothing of value. Music is usually the predominant element in an album. There are singers who have strong spirits and personalities; some of them do ensure that the power of the music does not override the strength of their spirit, and a few, precious few, lead lives that are close enough to God for the expression of their spirit to be also an expression of God's Spirit. One who comes to mind is Keith Green. Whether you like his musical style or not, listen to his recordings and see what hits you the hardest, the music or the message.

Remember, though, that even a great message will only communicate itself if there is conviction of spirit behind the performance. Good lyrics are not, in themselves, enough. The principle is clear in the Bible that "the letter kills, but the Spirit gives life" (2 Cor 3:6). Even the "letter" of scripture (to which Paul is referring) can be dead, unless God's Spirit is speaking it. The use of scriptural lyrics is not in itself enough reason to justify a song, a singer, or a style.

Christian Communication

We have noted that there is no such thing as Christian music; there are only Christians who play music. When a musician is a vessel for God's Spirit, and that Spirit is manifested in their singing or playing, then that is the closest we get to a definition of Christian music. But we cannot say that Christian words make a Christian song, or that a Christian performer will automatically produce Christian music. It's the expression of the Spirit of God that counts for everything.

Statistics, if they can be trusted, suggest that the words we say only account for 7% of what we really communicate to others. 38% is communicated by *how* we say the words, and 55% by more subconscious means of communication - body language, eyes, demeanour. However reliable (or otherwise) such statistics may be, it is generally accepted that the words we say are of relatively little effect if they are not backed up by spirit and conviction. If this is true of non-Christians, how much more is it necessary for Christians, whose great privilege and purpose is to express the Spirit of God?

Modes of expression and the use of body language are sometimes subjected to analysis and taught as a "method" in seminars, in the hope of turning out speakers or singers with more conviction and communicative power. That, to me, is just so much futile effort, and will certainly never produce genuine communication and conviction. If your lifestyle backs up your words, and you really mean and live your message, you will naturally say things "the right way", and the conviction will be there. But if you are only acting and putting on the right outward behaviour to impress your audience, that is sheer hypocrisy.

Worship Or Performance?

Sometimes performance and corporate worship become confused. I was once part of a "worship team" leading a conference, and we decided to introduce the people to a new chorus right at the start of a meeting, as they were coming in. As we rehearsed the bright, up-tempo praise chorus, we were enjoying playing together, and soon we had an arrangement that sounded great to us. We felt pleased that we were producing such a good sound, and sure enough, as we played to the people at the beginning of the meeting, it made an impression. Some people commented on how much they enjoyed it. But afterwards one of the main speakers at the conference spoke to us privately. In no uncertain terms, he told us what he felt. "You are a worship team" he said, "and you are supposed to be leading the people into worship. But you were *performing* up there. It just sounded like you were showing off your talents". Hackles rose among the musicians! I had to admit that the speaker was right, but his comments smarted. At the time, some of the music team objected to what he had to say, but the general feeling afterwards was that we had learned a timely lesson. Our egos had become involved in the music, and we needed that rebuke to expose us. Thank God for the people who are prepared to do that.

Chapter 25

Spiritual Meaning In Music

I'm lost in music
Caught in a trap
No turning back
I'm lost in music

Sister Sledge, "Lost in music"

At the beginning of this book we asked some fundamental but perplexing questions. What is music? Why does it affect us? How does it affect us?

We have seen that music has spiritual as well as physical aspects. We have examined many of the powers that can work through music: evocative, imaginative, hypnotic, addictive, expressive and impressive, manipulative, and so on; and we have seen that these powers can either be used or abused.

We have looked at musical styles and observed that style is rooted in spirit. We have considered the development of the arts and culture as part of the world system, and examined the origins and destination of that system, along with its inspirational guiding forces. We have noted that the values and ethos of the modern myth are powerfully projected onto society through the compelling power of image, and that music plays a major role in this strange, partly subliminal, subconscious work. Finally, we have seen that the effectiveness of music in God's work depends primarily and essentially on the quality of the musician's spiritual relationship with God.

With this background, I want to take another look at those first questions: How does music affect us? What happens when we listen to music?

Meaning And Response

When I listen to a piece of music, I respond in different ways and in differing degrees to different things in the music. There are various types of response, and various sorts of meaning in the music. I respond to the beauty of harmony, the tonality of consonance and dissonance, tension and resolution which forms the foundation of all western music and reflects the patterns of harmonics found in nature. (For more on this, see Appendix.) The beauty of melodic structure, the craft and skill with which the music is performed, the harmonizing effect of the musicians playing together in unity, all contribute to the meaning of the music and my response to it. I wince if the music is off key or out of rhythm. I get pleasure if it's in tune and together.

One of the chief types of meaning and response is emotional. We all know that music can move and manipulate our emotions very powerfully. The emotion could be aggressive (depending for its effect on loud volume, driving rhythm, angularity and dissonance) or it could be soothing (utilizing gentle, warm sounds and consonant harmonies, and putting the emphasis on lyrical melody and harmony rather than rhythm). Music can stir heroic sentiments or sensuous passions. It can make you happy or sad, subdue you or excite you. In short, music encompasses and expresses just about the whole range of human emotions. When it is combined with other media (as in films, for example) its emotional effect is further heightened. Our feelings respond, immediately, consciously and obviously, to these elements in the music.

The Hidden Work

But beyond this level of response lies something deeper. There is another level of meaning, the level at which our spirits respond subconsciously. As we respond to the spiritual meaning and message of the music, a hidden but powerful effect is at work upon our spirits, for better or worse.

This is where music does its most potent work. It is here that the spirit behind the style asserts itself and makes its mark. It is here that subliminal suggestions become effective, and here that image works its peculiar charms. It is at this level that messages are preached into people's subconscious, that values are formed and changed, and people are subtly conformed to the image and its message. It is this that makes a piece of music so mysteriously attractive, so strangely compelling. It is here, too, that God can use music powerfully. It is here that a musician expressing the Spirit of God can be a means of blessing and real change in people's lives - not just temporary changes in feelings but deeper spiritual changes in attitudes and motives, with lasting effects. It is here that a Christian life lived in close relationship with God bears fruit. This is the level at which true ministry happens.

Because this is a hidden, subconscious work, it is difficult to describe and evaluate. Many people are not even aware of its existence. But it is known by its results. Like the reaction of sub-atomic nuclei triggering an explosion of immense power, the subtle, unseen effects of this type of spiritual meaning in music can cause massive upheavals and changes in the minds and hearts of men and women.

A qualifying statement needs to be made at this point. Different people react with different degrees of sensitivity. Each person has their own degree of response. Some respond more to one "meaning", others more to another. But having said that, just as most people like music (proving that they are sensitive to its effects) so most people have at least some degree of sensitivity to spiritual effects. We are all spiritual beings.

"My Music"

We open ourselves up to music in exactly the same way as we do to people. We hear some music and we react inwardly. We like it. We "warm to it". Thus we open ourselves up to it. We let our barriers down. We begin to identify with the music. We recognise that this is a friend. It helps us or soothes us or excites us or "does something for us". We don't have to understand what it does. Music lovers aren't inclined to be analysts, any more than two people in love are concerned with analysing the nature of what has happened to them. What has undoubtedly happened (in both cases) is that a relationship has started. This is why people talk about a certain style as being "my music". It's something they identify with. The music has become a familiar friend - might we even say "a familiar spirit"?

Music is spiritual food. It feeds the spirit with things that only the spirit understands. "Deep calls unto deep". In a realm that goes beyond transient feelings, it comforts them, uplifts them and gives them a sense of security. They feel at one with the music and its message. Its image is their image. Its values are their values. The music acts as a former of thought and opinion. The music and/or the words appeal, not to the intellect (the logical, conscious thought), but to the subconscious, intuitive spiritual mind. Spirit is talking to spirit.

In the end, the unity we feel with what we call "my music" exists because the music is exerting a powerful influence upon our subconscious mind, even controlling us to some extent. It is our acceptance of this music and our identification with it that gives it this power. We have seen how addictive music can be, and addiction means you are being controlled to some extent. The lyrics quoted at the beginning of this chapter sum up these effects: "I'm lost in music / Caught in a trap / No turning back..." The music becomes a drug experience, an experience that controls you. Music is the controller, you are lost in it. Music is the power, you are "caught" in its spell. The pull to go deeper is always there. You can only keep on taking more of the drug. It's beyond your control. But this is an addiction people are happy to live with. As the same song says: "I won't give up my music / No way, no how!" (There's that phrase again: "my music".) No-one wants to give up what is theirs, what is close to them, what they identify with. It has become a part of them.

Life Experiences

I know what this is like. For years I was "lost in music". "My music" was mostly classical. It certainly exerted a powerful hold over me. Of course I was never conscious of it doing so in a negative sense, because musicians are encouraged (at least implicitly) to let music have a hold over them. Otherwise, how will they become good musicians? What else will motivate them to the years of patient practice they need to perfect instrumental technique? The effects of the drug, however, make it all worthwhile. I know the pleasure it gives. I know the "familiar spirit" syndrome.

I also knew what it was like to occasionally be without music for longer than I'd like to be. It wasn't a pleasant experience! The real world was harsh, cold, grey and boring. As soon as I was back to "my music" I was happy again. I had back my comforts, I had back something I identified with, something that motivated me, something that gave me security, the feeling that I was somebody and that I was a part of something.

I know, too, how music can affect the mind with the values of image and myth. For years, although I was nominally a Christian, I found it very hard to come to terms with people who made "black and white" statements. Clear-cut absolute truth was very hard for me to accept. I always objected inside. Something within me retorted, "It's not as simple as that!" Black and white was always turned to grey in my mind. The music fostered and nurtured this relativistic worldview. My experience since that time has confirmed that my mind used to be a very different place, confused and, for want of a better word, "fuzzy". Thoughts and values were indistinct, blurred, misty. My mind was jam-packed full of all sorts of random ideas, some of them contradictory, all of them conspiring to make me unable to think clearly and straight. What the bible calls a "sound mind" (2 Tim 1:7) is not a very common thing. Many times after I became a committed Christian I was aware of this "fuzziness" in my mind; it seemed that, as God was dealing with me and extracting me from the web I had become entangled in, I gradually became more aware of what my mind was really like. Slowly, things changed; the relativistic thinking disappeared; clear truth and absolute statements were no longer abhorrent to me. But this was only after God had dealt with me and got the effects of the music out of my system. My mind needed slowly renewing, weaning away from the spirit of the world.

Tubular Bells - The Spiritual Message

When Mike Oldfield's album "Tubular Bells" came out, I was among the many with whom it became a firm favourite. I used to listen to it a lot as a young Christian. Several years later, I met another Christian who had heard Tubular Bells - just a short snippet of it on the radio - but this person's reaction was completely different to mine. A tremendous sense of evil had come over her, and she had to immediately switch the radio off. She had no idea what the music was. She didn't know (and neither did I) that it was used for the film "The Exorcist". Perhaps I would have thought differently if I'd known that. Perhaps I would have felt differently if I'd known that Tubular Bells would go down in history as the first major album of New Age music.

As it was, I think if any Christian had challenged me about Tubular Bells, I would have been very defensive. I would have pointed out, as Christians are forever doing, that there was nothing wrong with its content (after all, there were no lyrics - it was a purely instrumental album), and its style, of course, couldn't be faulted - it was pleasant, tuneful music to listen to. It is an instructive lesson to learn that the absence of lyrics and the presence of pleasing melody and harmony do not automatically give a piece of music a "clean bill of health". Style, content, and even emotional effect are all different manifestations of the cause, the source, the root. That root is spirit - the hidden element. That's what counts, and what dictates the real meaning and effect of the music.

By the time I met the friend who told me of this experience, my attitude had changed. I recognised the dangers. But it made me think back to the times when I played that record over and over. There was certainly something compellingly attractive about it. It was, in a sense, food to my spirit. Who knows how much it contributed to the shaping of my thoughts and even my attitudes? The music does this. It appeals to something beyond feelings - to the motives and attitudes deep down at the centre of our being, to spiritual qualities.

The Positive Side

There is a positive side to this, of course. I have for some years played my own instrumental music in ministry in churches and prisons. Many times people have said how much the music has moved them or even what a wonderful spiritual experience it has given them. But often I have been uneasy - my suspicions are that many of these people are responding purely on the level of feelings. And that's alright;

there's nothing wrong with feelings. It's just that I want the music to do something more. An emotional response won't last long. I want there to be a spiritual work done; for spirit to communicate with spirit; for God's Spirit to be expressed through me as I express myself in music, and for deep, lasting changes to take place in the minds, hearts and attitudes of others. I don't generally expect people to feel an immediate reaction or change within them; I expect a slow, subconscious process to start as the Spirit of God does His work in that person.

If, by God's grace, this happens, I don't expect those people to necessarily associate the changes taking place in them with my ministry. Often we are not even conscious of the change in ourselves. Spiritual change tends to happen despite us, without us noticing. We meet someone we've not seen for a while and they say, "You've changed!", and we think, "I have?!" It's a surprise to us, because it's a subconscious work in our hearts. Emotional changes are easy to spot - they are dramatic experiences of feeling, like a sudden burst of flame. But they die down and disappear as quickly as they came. This, of course, is a very common thing in music, which appeals so much to our feelings. However, the subconscious spiritual changes are much more subtle, much less easy to see in the short term, but much deeper and more powerful in the long term, and much more permanent. This is the goal of genuine music ministry (and indeed of all ministry), and of course it depends entirely (as I have been at pains to stress in the last few chapters) on the quality of our relationship with God, our closeness to Him, and our brokenness.

This deep, subconscious spiritual meaning is the hidden secret of music's power and effectiveness, for good or for evil. Because of this spiritual dimension, music can play a major role in fostering a proud, arrogant and haughty spirit

- or a tender, humble and broken spirit - influencing us in our innermost being, and deeply colouring our view of ourselves, others and the world around us. We are seeing the spiritual results of the music explosion every day, whether we realise it or not, in our own lives and the lives of the people around us.

Chapter 26

Seven Dangers - A Personal Check-list

Most of us follow our conscience as we follow a wheelbarrow. We push it in front of us in the direction we want it to go.

Billy Graham

No challenge, however strong, is of any use unless it has practical consequences. Reading a book or listening to a preacher and agreeing with what they say is meaningless. Being convicted by what they say is also meaningless, unless that conviction leads you to do something, to change, to act.

So this chapter is a practical check-list for you, highlighting some of the dangers we all face from being involved with the power of music. It is for you to test yourself. If you feel these issues have nothing to say to you, or have no influence on your life, that's fine. On the other hand, if the cap fits, wear it, and decide what you need to do as a result. But do be realistic. Each one of us has to face these issues, and to claim that none of them affect us would simply be kidding ourselves. We need to be both truthful and practical.

1. Independence and Individualism

As we have seen, the spirit of independence is at the root of culture. Independence and individualism are at the root of rebellion, and outright rebellion is at the root of some music. When we listen to music, we can, without realising it, be feeding that independent nature - whether it manifests itself as independence from God, independence from authority or independence from the church. If you find yourself defending your listening or concert-going or playing with a "why shouldn't I" attitude, that is symptomatic of independence. If you find you are always quarrelling with your worship group in church, that is probably also because of independence. We all have an independent streak, and we all have to deal with it, but we don't need to feed it! Check out your attitude to the music you play and listen to. Does it foster that spirit of independence in you?

The opposite of independence is *dependence* - dependence on God, first of all; which, for musicians, means not trusting in your own skills too much, but in everything you do, acknowledging your dependence on God. It also means bringing yourself and your music - the music you listen to and the music you play - to God's altar, and letting Him search you out and tell you what you should and shouldn't be doing - and being ready to let go of anything, anything at all, if He tells you to. Being dependent on God means accepting and submitting to what He says to you. This all depends, of course, on you having a personal relationship with God where He does talk to you and you know His voice. That is essential.

Dependence also means submission to authority and to other people's wishes, whether parents, pastors, worship leaders or friends. A submissive spirit is the great antidote to independence. Learn to be kind and forgiving. Musicians can be very sarcastic and cutting about other people's standards and tastes. That's not a godly attitude. James' words on earthly and heavenly wisdom speak to us here (Jas 3:13-18). Those who have heavenly wisdom have a beautiful quality: they are "easily entreated" (v 17). They yield easily; they submit, and don't resist. This goes against the grain for a lot of musicians, because we always think that we know what's right in terms of style and taste. The root of this arrogant attitude is independence.

I speak from experience! I used to despise the music I heard in church, and the musicians who played it. Actually, although I would have never admitted it to myself, I despised most musicians except myself, because my taste was always perfect when other people's seemed so sadly lacking, and I always knew the right thing to do when everyone else didn't have the first clue. In brief, everyone except me was a fool! God had to do a lot of work to get this arrogant, independent attitude out of me. I needed humbling. I had to learn, gradually, how to be submissive, easily entreated and generous in spirit - and I don't think I've finished learning yet!

2. Inundation and Indulgence

Our society is inundated with music. The sheer amount of music available to so many people, from so many sources, in so many different styles, is staggering. What should our response be as Christians to the force of this "music explosion"?

The lack of references to music in the New Testament (see Chapter 27) seem to indicate that we are now making music a far higher priority than the early Church did. How do we come to terms with this? Are we guilty of just being pulled along by the trends of the world?

As always, the best solution for us as Christians is to have our own trend - in the opposite direction. There is a lot of talk about "counter-culture" in some Christian circles; but generally this "counter-culture" turns out to be no more than a "parallel culture", going in exactly the same direction as the main culture, imitating its values and sharing its inspiration, but with the name "Christian" tagged on.

The differences between the world's culture and today's Christian "counter-culture" are mostly cosmetic. We have become masters at "borrowing and Christianizing". We keep a keen ear out for what the world is doing, and when we hear something we like, be it celtic folk-rock, techno-thrash or classical guitar, we plagiarize the style wholesale, dress it up in Christian vocabulary and put it out on a Christian record label, and - hey presto! - a "counter-culture" is born. Or so we like to believe.

As regards the amount of time we devote to music in our luxurious, music-saturated society, the solution is *abstemiousness*, the opposite of indulgence. We are, after all, called to deny ourselves if we want to be followers of Christ (Mt 16:24). In an indulgent age, we are called to fast. In a selfish age that says "Look out for number one", we are called to mourn and reach out to the lost and suffering. In an age of gross financial indulgence and greed, we are called to give sacrificially. If Jesus tells us to deny ourselves such good and natural things as food, should we not also be careful to err on the side of abstemiousness with music, lest we follow the world and make music our idol?

When you have a moment, sit down and work out roughly how many hours per day or per week you spend either listening to or playing music. There is always a danger of excess when it comes to any of the desirable and attractive things in life; and really, as Christians, we ought to covet the chance to put it all to one side for a while - perhaps to "fast from music" for a few days. You might be surprised at how much you miss it. You may even suffer some withdrawal symptoms! But you might also be surprised at the beneficial effects of "cleaning out" your mental and spiritual system.

If all we do is share the same values and lifestyle as the rest of society (i.e. we spend the same number of hours per week doing the same things), then that doesn't really say much for our Christianity, and it's hardly a witness to the world. We do have to be different. Christianity turns all society's values upside down, and the values of God can only be manifested in the practical detail of our lives and lifestyles.

3. Idolatry

All musicians tinker with idolatry at some time. An idol is anything that is the object of worship or excessive devotion. An idol is also a powerful and influential force. Music beckons each of us with exactly these impressive credentials. When it succeeds in drawing us with its charms, we soon find ourselves hooked. If we are musicians, the hook is stronger, because we now literally have power at our fingertips. Music is a generous god, freely bestowing its powers upon mortal mankind. It is difficult to resist the lure of such a powerful force. And why should we? Music can sit secure on its throne in our hearts without a rival - until God comes into our lives.

And it is precisely because God has come into our lives, that music, in so much as it is an idol to us, becomes a problem. We must understand clearly that music is not a bad thing, and neither is having an idol. The problem is that we have a jealous God who desires to be our only Idol! He will not share His glory with another. It is not a question of whether the "other" is good or bad, but of whether it is an idol, a rival for our allegiance to God. For most Christian musicians, an idol is what music sooner or later threatens to become; and the same goes for those who are just listeners.

The comparison between a "big venue" rock concert, and the rituals and festivals of pagan idol-worship, has been made so many times that it has become a hackneyed analogy. But it reveals the truth that idolatry is the common root of both events. The idolising of music is one of the most disturbing aspects of the 20th century "music explosion". The same is true whether the audience is "freaking out" at a rock concert or sitting enraptured in a concert hall listening to a symphony. The game has become serious. Gone are the days when a piece of music was entitled "Divertimento" (diversion), a piece of background entertainment to accompany the social pleasantries of a dance or banquet. There, the music was merely an appendage; now it is the sole focus of attention.

A Simple Test

For Christians, music, used either in a worship context or just for listening, may present a most captivating image. It can be enthralling, stunningly beautiful, exciting, inspiring. We have seen how many and how powerful are its effects. All of us, as Christians, need to ask: Does this music have power over me? Can I do without it? Am I hooked on music? Am I using my music to serve God, or using God to serve my music?

There are a few simple tests we can give ourselves. One, as suggested earlier, is "fasting from music" for a few days. Another test can be applied when you have been listening to, singing or playing music. Spend a little time consciously reflecting on the music and its effects, and ask yourself a few pertinent questions: Do you feel closer to God as a result of the music? Have you learned or experienced more of God? Has it inspired you to pray, worship, evangelize, fast, seek God? Do you feel exalted or humbled as a result of it? Did the music appeal to your ego and self-esteem, or are you more aware of the convicting presence of God's Spirit, calling you away from self and towards Him? Was the music a vehicle for God's character, His nature, His holiness?

Perhaps some of these questions may be difficult or impossible for you to answer. But in some cases they may be a very useful test. If you spend some time reflecting in this way, you many start to notice a difference between certain times of worship/listening and others. Learning to discern is important. (It is also important not to be too self-analytical, so these sort of tests ought not to be taken too far. They are meant to prompt intuitive responses, not hours of introspective mental torture!) But whatever you do, don't do what most people do - don't just take it for granted that you have got your priorities right. Ninety-nine per cent of the time, we tend to just presume that our priorities are right; in fact, the very thought that anything else might be the case seems preposterous. "Of course I love God more than music!" we say. "Of course music is not as important to me as God!" But please let us not take that for granted. It's unwise (as well as conceited!) to say those sort of things without consideration and self-examination. We should regularly be bringing ourselves before God and asking Him to search our hearts and try our motives (as David did in Psalm 139:23-24), and expose us where we are at fault. We need to know ourselves, as well as knowing God.

Sometimes a genuinely beneficial spiritual experience can be produced by something which may later become a source of idolatry. Two examples occur to me; one is from scripture and the other from my own experience.

Nehushtan

In Numbers 21, the story is recorded of how God sent "fiery serpents" because of Israel's rebelliousness. When Moses interceded for the people, God told him to make a bronze serpent and put it on a pole. Whenever a person was bitten, if they looked at the bronze serpent, they would be healed. But in the days of King Hezekiah, the children of Israel burnt incense to this same bronze serpent - it had become an idol, because of its association with God and miraculous power. The association was a fair one; it had indeed been used by God. But now Hezekiah saw that the worship of it was misconceived, and he dealt ruthlessly with the situation: "he broke in pieces the bronze serpent that Moses had made ... and he called it 'Nehushtan' (which means 'a piece of bronze')" (2 Kings 18:4). Hezekiah realized that what had once carried God's anointing and power was in itself only a bit of metal. Perhaps there are things in our lives - things to do with music - that have at one time been used by God, but now have become idols to us and need "breaking in pieces"?

A Personal Experience

A while ago, I personally went through a particularly hard time. Circumstances and problems conspired to put me under tremendous pressure. I was greatly troubled, and I didn't know even how to begin to pray. A friend had, just that day, sent me a copy of a tape for which I had done one of the music arrangements. I listened to my arrangement, and it had turned out well. But the next piece on the tape was a classical instrumental piece by Bach. I have worked as a professional classical musician for years, and I am familiar enough with classical music; and I'm not someone who regards classical music as being any more or less godly than any other style. But this piece (which I had heard many times before in similar arrangements) was played so beautifully and expressively (by Christians), that instantly I felt God's presence, and it broke me and melted me completely. That music, for me at that time, was a vehicle for God's Spirit. God did a wonderful work of healing and restoration in my life. This was a precious and treasured experience for me.

However, the problem was that I then started to treasure the music as well as the experience, and I fell into the old trap (albeit subconsciously) of trying to recreate the experience by playing the music. In no time at all I had turned the situation on its head and begun to idolize the music, listening to how beautiful it was and craving its effects. It was ministering to my ego, no longer to my needs. When I recognized what I was doing, I knew that I had made the same mistake as the children of Israel with the bronze serpent. The music had to be "broken in pieces", because it was only music. I didn't smash the tape up! - but at the time of writing, I haven't listened to it again since.

We must not allow music to gain power over us. The Christians who played the music on that tape were using music in a beautiful and proper way - a real and powerful expression of their spirits. The problem of idolatry was not theirs, but mine. It was my motives in listening that became corrupted.

We must not be slaves to anything. That's what Christian freedom means - that my only need is God. Anything else I can do without. As Paul says, "All things are lawful for me, but I will not be brought under the power of any" (1 Cor 6:12).

The same goes for instruments as for music generally. A flute, guitar or drum kit can also be "gods of wood and metal". I trained as a classical violinist, and my violin certainly was my "little wooden idol". I gave it the best sort of worship - all my time, energy, desires and ambitions. Each of us as Christian musicians ought to bring our attitude towards our own instrument, and our own talent, before the Lord, and lay it on God's altar. We must each go through this process personally, allowing God to hold absolute sway over everything in our lives. If you can't let go of your instrument and give it up for God, you shouldn't be on a platform ministering. It's as simple and as drastic as that.

The Importance Of Prayer

One of the problems with idolatry is that you can be unaware of its presence in your life. King Jehu of Israel smashed the idol-worship of Baal in one bold, uncompromising stroke (2 Kings 10:18-28). But the next verse tells us that "Jehu did not depart from the sins of Jeroboam ... that is, the golden calves that were in Bethel and Dan" (v 29). Why did Jehu not put and end to this idolatry also? He was obviously not lacking in strength or zeal, and he was no "menpleaser". I believe it is quite possible that Jehu did not even realise the golden calves were idols. They had been around as part of Israel's worship for so long that he perhaps took them for granted. And so it can be with us. There are many, many things in our way of life that we take for granted and never think about! For this reason, we need to pray that God will reveal and expose the hidden idolatries in our hearts. God is well able to do this. My own experience tells me that He *will* do it, if we will ask Him to.

4. Impression

We have talked a good deal about the principle of expression and impression. Now we need to apply it practically and personally, and ask ourselves: Am I, consciously or subconsciously, seeking to use music as an "impressive" device in the wrong sense?

There are several tell-tale signs which can help to show us when our attitudes to music are beginning to go awry. For example:

1. When you hear the music, you immediately get a great "buzz"; you think "Oh, I love this song" - if it's in a time of church singing, you're up on your feet straight away at the sound of the music. When we say "I love this song", we often really mean, "I love this music, I'm hooked on this music, this music gives me a great experience". We need to remind ourselves that Jesus should be the object of our love, not songs about him.

2. As the music starts, you find yourself listening to it, taking it in (or being taken in by it), focused on it, enjoying it. In such a situation the words can tend to take second place, and the music, rather than the words, or God, becomes the inspiring element. If this is the case, it is music, rather than God, that you are worshipping. Many Christians, believing sincerely that they are worshipping God, are in fact "worshippers of worship".

3. Cheering and applause at the end of some choruses have almost become part of the stock-in-trade of lively praise and worship sessions. I personally believe that this tends to be a response to the music far more than a response to God. People would perhaps not agree with this; but they don't clap and cheer after a prayer. Why not? Maybe it's just custom; but if you take note of where such "applause" comes, you're likely to find that it is invariably after a chorus that has a good musical "feel".

4. When the music stops, your feelings stop. Your attitude of praise or worship ceases when the music ceases, and resumes when the music starts up again. This is a sure sign that impression, rather than expression, is at work.

People who tend towards impression are often dependent on music: people who tend towards expression are more liable to express themselves through other non-musical means (e.g. prayer) with equal satisfaction. People who tend towards impression also tend to be experience-centred - they need, and seek for, experiences in order to enable them to express themselves to their satisfaction. "Expressers", conversely, have no need of an initial experience - the source and root of their expression is permanently within them.

I remember being at a conference right at the beginning of my Christian life, where one of the worship leaders would just say, without any preparation, "Let's all praise God". The roof would nearly lift off with the praise! No music, often no singing at all, just what the Bible calls "shouts of acclamation". This really was expression, not impression. It didn't need "working up", it was already there, in the people. No "mood" or "atmosphere" needed to be "impressed" on us; the people were only waiting for their opportunity to express themselves.

5. Sometimes it can happen that while listening to music you become acutely aware of your own feelings - often your feelings about God or towards God. These feelings can sometimes seem very profound. You may feel you are very close to God and that you have a great love for God. Such feelings are deceptively lofty, but they can actually be just a form of self-exaltation, brought about by the emotional introspection that comes from being "impressed" with music. You may feel you love God, but actually you may be more concerned with yourself than with God. It may be your love for God that pleases you and gives you a warm glow in your heart. This could be self-glorification in Christian guise, feeding the flesh and breeding pride.

These "tell-tale signs" are things we each need to look out for personally, whether we are listeners or performers. Certainly, if you are either a performer or a composer, you should ask yourself: When I play or write music, is my purpose to create a beautiful atmosphere, stunning sound or captivating experience - or is it designed to be a foundation for people to express themselves? Is its purpose primarily to be evocative (impressive), or expressive?

5. Introspection

All the dangers we have listed are linked; the experiences

of indulgence, idolatry and impression all overlap each other, and where one is present, the others tend also to be present in a measure. To an extent they feed off each other. Hence the above comment about "emotional introspection" resulting from impression.

Some people are naturally introvert, reserved or inward looking. As a personality trait, introversion is not a bad thing, but introspection (preoccupation with one's own mind and thought processes) is a dangerous thing. The thing that makes it dangerous is *self*. Self-centredness is, of course, just as evident in extroverts as in introverts, although it manifests itself differently. Introverts usually display selfishness by turning in on themselves. An introspective person lives in his or her own world. Everything centres around them and their experience. The outside world seems hostile and unfriendly. The temptation is to crawl further into your own isolated world, and music suits this; in fact it paves the way for it. I described in Chapter 4 my own experience of becoming trapped in a "fantasy world" through the wrong use of imagination and impression.

Introverts tend generally towards impression rather than expression. For them, impression is a particular danger. Extroverts are more likely to be "expressers", less conscious of their inward state of mind. Fantasy is more harmful to introverts, because their sense of imagination tends to be less well grounded in reality. To the introvert, music can present a whole imaginary world into which they can retreat and indulge in brooding introspection.

The way your thoughts and imaginations run when you listen to music should tell you whether you are susceptible to introspection. If you are, then you should be particularly careful in your listening habits and musical involvement. I think you would be wise to err on the side of abstemiousness. Introspection is dangerous because it tends to cut you off from the real world and trap you inside your own mind and emotions. It feeds off impression, and it feeds your sense of fantasy. It separates you from other people and their needs. It fosters self-centredness, self-pity, and self-preoccupation, and as Christians we have a mandate to put God and others first, and therefore to not allow music to feed our taste for introspection.

6. Image

We have explored at some length the subject of image in our culture, and the way values are sold to us through image by the media and the arts. We have seen how the moral, ethical and philosophical values of the "myth" which is at the basis of our culture are opposed to the values of Christianity, and how these values are at the basis of much of the music we listen to.

This presents us as Christians with a major challenge. We need to establish a genuine alternative - not because we need a means of "getting into the world" or imitating culture, but because we recognise that the values of the world and the values of God are opposites. We need today to be alert to the danger of our value system and way of thinking being infiltrated by the world's cultural values of fantasy, image and myth: and it is important that we understand the difference between the two systems. That means understanding the world's way - how the media make use of image and fantasy to put across their values, what exactly those values are, and how they differ from God's values.

We then need to understand the principles of the way God works (through expression, not impression; through truth, not fantasy and image; through people, not "things" and "forces"; through brokenness, weakness and humility, not through human power, aggressive hype and self-exaltation); and we need to apply these principles to the way we work.

The "powers" of impression, indulgence, evocation and idolatry all play a large part in the creation of "image" in music. We must make sure that we do not abuse these powers, or we could become guilty of trapping ourselves, and other people, in the culture of image. We need to ask ourselves how much we may have already taken on board of the values and principles of that culture, and we need to root them out wherever we find them. Perhaps more importantly, we need to ask God to show us where the world's values have entered into our listening/playing habits, and be ready to deal with what God may point out to us as we seek Him in prayer.

7. The Use Of Imagination

Imagination and fantasy are related, but they are not the same. Every musician must use imagination in order to create and compose, but no musician need use fantasy. Fantasy is the abuse of imaginative power. Fantasy is always false; it is the opposite of truth and reality. Imagination, on the other hand, is a legitimate power that can be used or abused. In discussing imaginative power (Chapter 4), I emphasized the abuse of the imagination to create fantasy. But there are clearly proper uses of imagination. I would distinguish two main types of "proper imagination":

1. Spontaneous Imagination

When you read a novel, every sentence has to be translated into a mental image in order for it to make sense to us. It is the imagination that creates these images, so that in our minds we spontaneously visualize a person or situation as described in the novel. In the same way, in everyday conversation, our minds are constantly visualising the things we are being told. As soon as someone says to you "I went to see so-and-so yesterday", you immediately have a picture of that person "in your mind's eye". This happens without us thinking about it. When we meet someone for the first time, we often think to ourselves "They're nothing like I imagined". That doesn't mean that we spent time consciously developing an image of what we expected that person to look like; it is simply part of the natural, spontaneous working of imagination that accompanies us through everyday life. Dreams, too, belong to this realm of subconscious, spontaneous imagination. As Christians, we use spontaneous imagination whenever we think of people as we pray for them. It is not something we consciously or deliberately do; in fact, consciously doing it can lead to a dangerous abuse of imagination.

2. Creative Imagination

We need to use imagination to be artistically creative. Every creation depends on the use of imagination. Everyone who has learned to be creative has been told, at some point, "Use your imagination!" That means: stretch your thinking. Apply your mind. Don't get stuck in a rut. Think of something different. It doesn't mean "fantasize". A gardener draws on creative imagination. There is no fantasy element in what he is doing; everything is real. But he uses creative imagination to make the best and most pleasing effects out of the materials he has. An architect does the same; he needs creative imagination to plan what he cannot yet see, and to produce a building that is different. But it is a real building in the real world. In this way we can see how fantasy differs from imagination. The fantasist creates something which is basically impossible, unreal and false. But the proper use of creative imagination is always firmly wedded to reality.

Jesus' parables use creative imagination. His hearers were expected to naturally visualize what He was telling them about, whether it be a field of wheat or a story about a father and son. Jesus was the creative one, using imaginary scenarios in order to make a point. But again, although the parables are imaginary (the story of the prodigal son is not historical fact), they are rooted in reality, in the sense that they could all have happened. Jesus was talking about real-life situations. There is no fantasy about it; it is all about real things, about realism and truth.

The principles that govern a Christian's use of creative imagination are twofold:

1. The imagined thing should be *grounded in reality* and related to real life, as Jesus' parables were; if it is not rooted in reality, it becomes fantasy, and contains that unreal element which can cause so much damage to the imaginative person's mind. How can we relate this principle to music? How can music be "rooted in reality?" I think that it all hinges around the purpose of the music. Expression is to do with reality; impression is generally to do with fantasy. This adds further weight to the idea that our musical creations should be the product of expression, not impression - because we want to say something, rather than because we like the sound of something.

2. The imagination should be used to create *a vehicle for truth*. It should be a means of making a point, a means of getting across a message, and that message must be truth. If there is no "point", then the imagination itself becomes the important aspect, and it can all too easily lead off into fantasy if there is no message of truth to grasp hold of. A song without a message becomes merely entertainment. Moreover, the message needs to be strong in order for it to get across, otherwise it will be the evocative beauty and aesthetic impression of the music that make the impact on us, rather than the truth of the message.

Sometimes creative imagination and fantasy become confused. This seems to be the case with the increasingly popular Christian fantasy novels which are allegories of truth. The setting of the novels is entirely fantasy, but the allegory is supposed to make a point about truth. Some people contend that Tolkien's "Lord of the Rings" is a Christian allegory. I would be prepared to argue that if it is, then the allegory is certainly rather obscure, and that, more importantly, the fantasy world created in the book is vastly more powerful that any allegorical statement of truth that Tolkien wanted to make. The thing that grips people who read Tolkien's work (and, I would suggest, most other fantasy/sci-fi novels) is not the allegory or the truth but the fantasy.

More disturbing still is the fact that fantasy novels such as *Lord of the Rings* and even C. S. Lewis' *Chronicles of Narnia* (in which the Christian allegory is far clearer) are regarded as essential reading for people involved in witchcraft, particularly what is known as "white" witchcraft. Why? Purely because of the power of the fantasy element. The occult draws people in through fascination with every kind of fantasy and unreality. Glimpses of "another world" in folk tales, myths and legends are powerful evocative forces, and music used in such a context (e.g. in films of fantasy novels, romantic opera, or instrumental music geared towards descriptive fantasy) only adds to the power of the fantasy.

Visualisation - The Abuse Of Imagination

Visualisation techniques have, in the last decade or so, found their way into Christian circles in the form of "guided imagery" used in counselling. The roots of visualisation are entirely occultic, and it is a dangerous misuse of the imagination. I mention it here only because music will sooner or later play a part in such techniques. Visualisation is used most commonly as a technique of "inner healing", whereby you are encouraged to deliberately imagine or visualize (for example) yourself meeting Jesus, and perhaps going with Him on a "journey" through past hurts and traumatic events in your life. The use of this sort of guided imagery has been encouraged by such popular Christian authors as C. S. Lovett, Calvin Miller and Richard Foster. But its roots are clearly confirmed by writers working in quite a different sphere. To briefly quote just two examples:

"Visualisation is one of the most potent and widely used techniques in psychic healing."[1]

"The technique of visualisation is something you ... must master if you are to make any progress at all in magic ... it enables us to build our own thought forms, contact those already in existence, and channel the elemental energy we need down onto the physical plane."[2]

I would advise you to steer well clear of anything that has to do with visualisation, the creation of fantasy situations and anything that encourages you to "conjure up" images in your mind, whether it is with the help of music or not. We are living in a dangerous age where all sorts of spiritual powers and forces are battling for recognition and supremacy, and the infiltration of occultic techniques into the church is alarming. Music will always be used as a tool for these techniques, because it is such an effective medium for spiritual communication; and its effect is heightened by the fact that so many Christians believe music is a wonderful gift from God, and too often make the glib equation: "If it's God's gift, it can't possibly be harmful." It is difficult to imagine a more dangerous supposition.

Notes

1. Bill Henkin and Amy Wallace, *The Psychic Healing Book: How to Develop your Psychic Potential* (Wingbow Press, 1982) p.43
2. David Conway, *Magic: An Occult Primer* , p.59, as quoted in Dave Hunt and T. L. McMahon, *The Seduction of Christianity* (Harvest House, 1985) p. 142

Chapter 27

What The New Testament Says About Music

Most people are bothered by those passages in Scripture which they cannot understand; but as for me, I always noticed that the passages in Scripture which troubled me most are those I do understand.

Mark Twain

I once picked up a interesting looking leaflet entitled "What the Bible says about infant baptism". A picture of a smiling baby graced the front cover. When I opened to the inside pages they were completely blank! Whatever your views on infant baptism, the tract made a point - there isn't much scriptural support for the practice. And I almost feel the same way about music. We have to search hard to find references to music in the New Testament, particularly references that would teach us anything about how music fits in with Christianity. Jesus never taught about it; Paul had virtually nothing to say to all the churches about it; and accounts of Christians actually singing or playing music are limited to two in the entire New Testament (Mt 26:30 and Acts 16:25; - both are instances of unaccompanied singing, and both, incidentally, occur in times of trouble).

There is far more evidence of music in the Old Testament, and much has been written about David's tabernacle and his appointment of musicians to the service of God. But we must not forget that this only happened at the time of David. When God first instituted the tabernacle in the wilderness through Moses, music certainly played a large part in the culture of the nation (as shown, for example, in the incident of the golden calf, which occurred at the same time). But strangely, there was no music in Moses' tabernacle. It was a silent place, and remained so for about 250 years. God designed it that way for a purpose, and whatever views we form as a result of our understanding of the Bible, we should bear in mind all the different stages and dispensations, and consider the significance of each.

As far as the New Testament is concerned, there are two main points that we need to note. Firstly, if the New Testament says hardly anything about music, music can hardly be essential to New Testament Christianity. That doesn't mean it is a bad thing; it only means it should not play a dominant role, and certainly not an vital role, in Christianity. Secondly, what the New Testament does say about music always has something to teach us. I have tried in this book to draw out some of the scriptural principles and apply them; but the Bible can always teach us more if we look hard enough, and if we genuinely want the truth. We can thus learn both from what the Bible does say, and from what it doesn't say.

The following is a list of the scriptures that refer to music in the New Testament. I have omitted references to angelic or heavenly music - that is a different subject, and even here we have popular misconceptions. For instance, we all know that the angels who appeared to the shepherds at Jesus' birth were a heavenly choir singing "Glory to God in the highest". But we're wrong! In fact it was not the choir but the army - "the heavenly host" - and they were "saying" (or perhaps shouting?), not "singing" (Lk 2:13,14).

I have also omitted mentions of "the trumpet of God", and oblique references in Jesus' parables (e.g. Mt 11:17, Lk 15:25), which can hardly be said to constitute biblical teaching about music.

Mt 26:30 "And when they [Jesus and the apostles] had

sung a hymn, they went out into the mount of Olives."

Acts 16:25 "And at midnight Paul and Silas prayed and sang praises to God: and the prisoners heard them."

1 Cor 14:7,8 "And even things without life giving sound, whether pipe or harp, unless they give a distinction in the sounds, how shall it be known what is being piped or harped? For if the trumpet give an uncertain sound, who shall prepare himself to the battle?"

1 Cor 14:15 "I will pray with the spirit, and I will pray with the understanding also: I will sing with the spirit, and I will sing with the understanding also."

Eph 5:18,19 "Be not drunk with wine, which is in excess; but be filled with the Spirit; speaking to yourselves in psalms and hymns and spiritual songs, singing and making melody in your heart to the Lord."

Col 3:16 "Let the word of Christ dwell in you richly in all wisdom; teaching and admonishing one another in psalms and hymns and spiritual songs, singing with grace in your hearts to the Lord."

Jas 5:13 "Is any among you afflicted? Let him pray. Is any merry? Let him sing psalms."

Rev 18:22 "And the voice of harpers, and musicians, and of pipers, and trumpeters, shall be heard no more at all in thee [Babylon]."

That's all there is. Are we overdoing it in the 20th century? Have we followed the world's trends, to our own hurt? You must come to your own conclusions - and take appropriate action.

Chapter 28

Questions People Ask

None so blind as those who won't see.

English Proverb

In this chapter I want to try and answer a few of the common problems that regularly crop up when "Christian music" is under debate. But first, a cautionary note. There are always going to be contentious issues, and we do need to be careful that in our debates we don't just end up fighting a war of opinions. Legalistic or biased answers will never satisfy anybody. On the other hand, sometimes the issues are brought up by legalistic and biased people! Jesus taught a salutary lesson in the way He answered His questioners. Rather than give them a direct answer to their question, He often answered the question that lay behind what they were asking; He was able to pin-point the root of their questions, and that often turned out to be an entirely different issue. We will try to do the same with these frequently asked questions.

1. "Why can't I be a Christian and listen to (...)"?

This is a popular question, occurring in many variations - you can fill in the blank with the "contentious style" of your choice! There is no doubt that certain styles of music arouse more controversy than others. To pick out two typical examples, young Christians are often heard to complain, "What's wrong with me listening to heavy metal?" or, "Why can't I be a Christian and play punk rock?" At first glance it looks as if the only answer to these questions is to start a debate about the values and merits (or otherwise) of the style in question. For those who are genuinely concerned to understand the principles behind the origins of styles, this book attempts to provide some answers. But when the questions are contentious, such debate usually only serves to heighten the contention. This is frustrating to both sides, but it shows up the fact that the real question has not been dealt with. The answer is not to engage in a complex debate about the style at all, but to highlight a much more basic underlying issue. All we need to do is ask, "Why does punk rock play such an integral part in your Christianity? Why are you so unwilling to live without it?" In other words, "Why aren't you free?"

That takes us to the root of the problem - freedom. The Bible says nothing about the relative merits of rap, classical or heavy metal. But it does talk about idolatry - the danger of things gaining a hold over us and trapping us. The apostle Paul summed it up when he said, "All things are lawful for me; but I will not be brought under the power of any" (1 Cor 6:12). The Bible talks about spiritual slavery or bondage, and contrasts that with truth and freedom. It talks about things that become rivals to God, and God's desire for unrivalled sovereignty in our lives. These are the principles that generally underlie the "contentious issues". True freedom means that nothing has a hold over you. I don't need to ask "Why can't I be a Christian and have green hair?", simply because I have no interest in having green hair! People may think I'm the one who is a slave because I don't do the things they do. They think that they are free because they do those things. But they don't realise that they do the things they do because they're compelled to, either by the lure of the things themselves or by their own selfishness (that most enslaving of characteristics). But the person who is free is not compelled by anything, except God's love. To the Christian who is free from idolatry, it is not a matter of "Why can't I do that?" Or "I am not allowed to do that", but of "I don't want to do that; I don't need that".

That's real freedom. But the Christian who has a problem with idolatry will find that the contentious issues will keep on raising their ugly heads, and the Christian life of such people often becomes one big fight to justify themselves. They may be right or they may be wrong; but it's usually their attitude that is the problem. They are really asking the wrong question, because they haven't realised that Christianity is not an "either/or" option. You can't actually have "Christianity plus" anything. Christianity is exclusive; it is one hundred per cent allegiance to Jesus. Everything else has to go. Paul summed up what Christianity meant to him in the words "I am crucified with Christ" (Gal 2:20). A crucified man has no alternative options in life! Jesus likewise warned his followers that they could not be His disciples unless they were willing to forsake all their possessions and affections, father and mother, and even their own life.

This kind of talk usually evokes the response, "But Jesus doesn't expect us all to just leave our parents and abandon everything we do!" Doesn't he? The fact is that the call of Jesus applies to all our natural affections and possessions in the world: love of music is only one of those things. Christianity leaves you only two options: either you have to leave those things, as a man does when he leaves the world and enters a monastery - or else those things have to leave you. Leaving the world is the easier option; but the world leaving you is the only genuinely Christian option. For you to abandon music and never play it or listen to it again is actually the easier option. The alternative is less straightforward - music has to leave you. That means you can use it and be involved with it, but it no longer has any hold or power over you. That is what being "in the world but not of it" means as far as music is concerned.

This is the attitude I have to take myself, because I still use music. I have to be perfectly content if I never played another note of music in my life, or never listened to another album. I don't mean that I should be so hard and unfeeling that I wouldn't feel sad, but that the prospect should not alarm or dismay me. I know I could be happy without it. If I couldn't be happy without it, that means my Christianity has become compromised - another god is beginning to vie for attention with the God who says "Thou shalt have no other gods besides Me". "My music" may come under the innocuous name of "hobby", "pastime" or "relaxation", but if music has not left me, if it still has a hold over me, it is still "Christianity plus ..." and "Christianity plus" is not Christianity!

2. "What's wrong with copying the world's styles?"

First there was country music. Then there was Christian country music. First there was rock; then there was Christian rock. First there was rave music; now we have Christian rave music. Christians seem to be the great imitators, forever jumping on the world's bandwagons. But, you may ask, what's wrong with copying the world's styles? Let me reverse the question. What's wrong with *not* copying the world's styles?! Why do we feel we have to? Have we no genuine musical inspiration of our own? And if, as I have suggested, style is always rooted in spirit, then if we as Christians are supposed to have a completely different spirit from the world, why are we borrowing styles that were birthed in the spirit of the world? In talking about counter-culture I have argued that we are guilty of taking on the world's ethos and values by our stylistic plagiarism. But even if it's not wrong to borrow other people's styles, surely it's a sad reflection. Why should we have to? Why is there no legitimate, different Christian style? Why don't we have anything new and original to say ourselves? Take that personally - take it as a challenge to your creativity and your Christian life, a challenge to get away from the values of the world and create something that genuinely represents and expresses the values of God.

3. "Why are Christian choruses so trite?"

This is one of a group of complaints which basically compare standards of music and musicianship in the Church with standards in the world. "Boring, predictable, repetitious, simplistic and trivial" is the way that some people perceive modern worship songs. There is certainly some justification, from the musical point of view, for the complaint that choruses are of a very limited and short-term musical appeal, and that their use of hackneyed chord sequences and unadventurous, repetitive melodic lines has conspired to keep the creativity of church worship at a consistently low level. But there is another side to the argument which we need to first consider.

I used to think that choruses were trite. I first became a Christian through the charismatic movement, and I came from a background of classical music training, so choruses immediately struck me as being banal and childish. I said to myself (and others), "That's not music!" The fact was, I despised choruses - until the day I realised that I'd been approaching it all from the wrong angle.

I have already spoken of the time when I first recognized the difference between expression and impression, and of the effect this had on my life and my attitude to music. Here, in the context of worship, I realized that these simple, basic tunes called choruses were never designed to be "impressive" music; they weren't meant to be great music, to give me a musical thrill, to improve my cultural awareness, or to lift me up to great aesthetic or spiritual heights. They were written and designed for me to express myself to God, and to express what I had received from Him. When I worshipped, and when I looked into my own heart, I found that, for all my classical education, I had no desire to express myself to God with profound music. When I reflected on what I had received from the Lord, I found that it was very pure, simple, and childlike, and so what I wanted to say to God was also pure, simple and childlike - and the choruses served that purpose for me perfectly. In many ways this principle still holds true. When I pray, I don't want to express myself to God with grand oratory and rhetoric, or in the sublime poetic language of a Shakespeare sonnet; my only desire is to talk honestly, openly, simply, and heart to heart with my Father. So it is with musical expression.

I realised that it was my pride, my musical snobbery, my sense of cultural elitism, and my desire to be "impressed" by music, that had caused me to despise worship music at first. So I think that before we make any judgements about the musical standards of choruses, we ought to bear our own attitudes in mind, and ensure that we are not harbouring pride in our hearts and approaching the whole subject (which, after all, is worship, not music) with the wrong attitude. Christianity and elitism have nothing in common.

A second simple answer to the people who find choruses trite is, "Why don't you come up with something better?" It is a poor sort of criticism that offers no alternatives!

However, these things aside, there are, it seems to me, some important and justifiable criticisms, many of which have more to do with the words than the music. For instance, there have been fears voiced that in the post-charismatic era we have created in our choruses a mini-culture of meaningless slogans, forever talking in vague generalities about love, glory, power, dominion, praise, and worship; that by selectively editing the Psalms (the "worship book" of the Old Testament) for our lyrics, we have effectively emasculated them, robbing them of their real power and humanity, and thus robbing our worship of any link with practical reality. Others feel, more seriously still, that the banality of our worship, both in musical and lyrical terms, is the reflection of a dangerously apathetic conformism, too uncritically willing to accept the new slogan of a catchy chorus as doctrinal truth without question. That bears more resemblance to the behaviour of brainwashed people than it does to the behaviour of the Body of Christ. Christianity is supposed to be rooted in reality, based on a personal, living relationship with God, and grounded in experiential truth - not in words, slogans and songs but in power, reality, and with the crucial aid of a "sound mind" (2 Tim 1:7).

Hymns and songs have, down the centuries, often been an important vehicle for teaching doctrine. One only has to think of Charles Wesley. It is also true, however, that hymns and choruses can just as easily be powerful vehicles for false doctrine. Heresy in a song is actually far more deceptive than heresy in a sermon. Our intellects are keenly alert to words on their own. We are far less alert, and far more likely to subconsciously take on board wrong doctrine, if it comes in the form of music, while we are carried away by some inspiring or stirring tune.

We must endeavour to be discerning about our worship. If there are things that disturb us, and if we have genuine, justifiable reasons for the way we feel, then we must voice those concerns, suggest alternatives (or even better, provide and teach alternatives) and take steps to ensure that we do not have any part in cultivating mindless worship, or a mindless church.

4. "Why Are Christian Musicians Second-Rate?"

A final question, closely related to the previous one, is "Why aren't standards of musicianship better in Christian circles?" In other words, "Why are Christian musicians regarded as second-rate, below the general standard of music in the world?" The question is usually linked with another: "Shouldn't musicians seek to excel for God?"

We have dealt elsewhere with the idea of "getting into the world for God" (Chapter 13) which I regard as a highly dangerous attitude for any Christian to take. We need to balance our views on the pursuit of excellence with responsible caution against the dangers of idolatry, indulgence, etc. Moreover, there is always the danger that in "seeking excellence" we are only kidding ourselves that we want to be "the best for God", when really what we want to do is compete with the world. But Christianity is not in competition with the world - it is in *opposition* to the world. If we genuinely want to excel for God, surely our priority, whether we are musicians or not, should be to excel in prayer, to excel in our relationship with God, to excel in the degree to which we manifest the fruit of His Spirit; and if we understand what ministry is about, we will know that the success of our music ministry, and the degree to which we truly excel in God's eyes, is the degree to which our lives bear fruit and manifest His life - not how much talent we have or how successful we become. When we've considered that, and when we've taken steps to press towards that mark, we can go on to consider the standards of our musicianship.

There is certainly much sub-standard and shoddy musicianship in worship groups and Christian music bands. And it is highly probable that those who are undisciplined in their musicianship will also lead shoddy, undisciplined spiritual lives. However, we cannot put the equation the other way round. Christians who have achieved musical excellence will not necessarily also lead disciplined, mature and responsible spiritual lives. The greater your talent, the greater the corresponding danger of your being pulled into idolatry. So many talented Christians fall prey to this, slowly but surely removing God from the centre of their lives, until His throne is finally usurped by the god of music, clothed in the sumptuous robes of "excellence", and revelling in pure self-glorification.

Chapter 29

If You Want To Be Used...

When Christ calls a man,
He bids him come and die.
Dietrich Bonhoeffer

Although I am a musician, music matters far less to me now than it did ten years ago. But God matters more. I am very happy with this state of affairs. My musical abilities have not gone downhill as a result of music becoming less important to me (I would like to think they have improved), but my attitudes towards music have radically changed.

If Christians put as much time and energy into seeking God as they do into music, I believe the Church would undergo a radical change for the better. I would dearly love to see Christian musicians getting more interested in the pursuit of God and cooling off a bit on the pursuit of music. Often the whole problem of music in Christianity boils down to the simple fact that we love music too much, and God not enough.

Indeed, this is a principle that we can apply not just to music, but to all created things, to everything that is in the world. No matter how good and beautiful such things may be in themselves, if we want to truly understand, enjoy and use them in the way God intended, we have to abandon them completely in our hearts. Every little tie that binds us to them will eventually make us slaves. Every attraction that pulls you towards music must be dealt with, or it will become ambition and idolatry. What begins as a desire eventually becomes a need or an addiction. All these ties must be broken. Only then can we be truly free. I have had to make many such breaks in the past with music, and each time I have been terribly afraid to "let go" of the music. I've felt that I will lose everything, that music will become dry and meaningless to me, that I will somehow lose a part of myself and be left with nothing. In the end I've found I have gained everything; I have lost only the dangerous ties that threatened to chain me to music and make me its slave - and in losing those, I have gained real freedom.

The Battle For Lordship Of Our Lives

The secret of using all of God's gifts is to never grasp them to yourself - indeed to never take them out of God's hands, but to take and use only what He offers, when He offers. Never hold onto them yourself, but let God retain the control.

The only way to receive is to give. In so many areas we find this principle at work. When we are in financial need, we struggle and sweat and pray - until we learn that the only way to receive is to give. "Give, and it shall be given unto you" (Lk 6:38). All the covetousness has to be wrenched out of our hearts. Even after we've learned the principles, we can abuse them, and start "giving in order to get". Covetousness sneaks back into our hearts in spiritual guise, because we still have our eyes on receiving, rather than giving; on money, and not on God.

In the same way we can learn all the right principles about music. But the aim of it all is not to gain knowledge, achievements and success in music, but to learn about God, His ways, His character, and how He wants to use you. Music is only a means to an end. So often it turns the other way round: the end becomes the means and the means becomes the end. Serving God becomes a means of being prosperous, healthy and happy, or a means of using your talent and fulfilling your own desires and ambitions.

We are constantly involved in a battle: the battle for

lordship of our lives. Jesus Christ seeks to win that battle and have complete lordship, sovereign rule. If we want to be used by God, the only way to success is through surrender. The only way to be exalted is to humble ourselves. The only way up is down. The only way to resurrection power is through death. God's ways are not our ways - but that doesn't mean that His ways cannot be understood. It just means that His ways run contrary to our ways. He always goes the way we think is foolish, the way of weakness, the way of brokenness, the way of surrender and humility. If we want to use music properly, the issue is actually about us being used. If we want to be used, we have to learn to go God's way - the way of the cross.

APPENDIX

Atonality

Atonality does not (yet!) come within the realm of most Christians' listening habits. Nevertheless, it is regarded as a valid musical language, and this begs a question which demands our consideration: Are tonality and atonality moral issues? Is there any sense in which we can call tonality good or godly? Conversely, can we in any way call atonality ungodly, evil or devil-inspired?

Like so many other new developments in music, atonality was treated with universal derision when it first appeared; but, unlike other developments, even now (nearly a hundred years after its beginnings in western music) most people find it meaningless and ugly. Why? Is there a spiritual reason? The question really boils down to this: Is the 12-semitone octave a God given "norm" or standard? If so, could we call any deviation from that "norm" a perversion of the godly standard?

Dispensing With The Gospel?

This is not the place for an in-depth study, and I only want to offer a couple of thoughts. The first thought came from a comment by Nigel Swinford, the founder of the New English Orchestra. Giving a series of talks on BBC Radio in 1994, he suggested that Schönberg[1], in introducing an alternative to tonality in the form of the "12-note system", had removed a crucial element from musical language - the element of tension and resolution which is at the centre of the language of tonality. This, he contended, was a subtle but spiritually significant move, because at one stroke it completely removed "the language of the gospel" from music. Tension and resolution are concepts which are at the heart of the gospel - the "tension" caused by the fall of man and sin being "resolved" by the grace of God in Christ, and finally by the restoration of all things in the new heaven and earth. Atonality suggests an alternative reading of the human condition: that there is no resolution, no answer, and no tension.

It immediately occurred to me that this "alternative reading" has a striking parallel in the values of the 20th century myth (for example, the existentialist/atheist viewpoint of no sin, no absolutes, and no God).

It should not be inferred from this that Schönberg was deliberately promoting these values; neither was it a conscious move on his part away from God or from the "language of the gospel". Schönberg's concern was primarily a musical one; he saw that conventional tonality had been stretched to its limits by the composers of the late 19th and early 20th centuries, and he was convinced that the time had come for an alternative system. Nevertheless, Schönberg was an unwitting participant in a trend which had a spiritual root - the trend away from God and His ways and values.

The most extreme of the first 12-note composers, Anton von Webern, (who was a theosophist, and was fascinated by Eastern religious thought) strove to write a piece of music which at no time suggested any tonality at all - music that created no "harmonic tension" of any sort but left the listener entirely in suspense, without any sense of key. He reckoned that if he could write such a piece, the listeners upon hearing it would be, in his own words, "saved by the Word". For Webern, atonality clearly had important moral and spiritual implications.

From this argument, we could perhaps conclude that tonality is "godly", but only in the sense that wheat or fruit trees are "godly" - because they reflect God's character in their nature, as Paul says (Rom 1:20). Creation talks "the language of the gospel". So although we can hardly call atonality ungodly in itself (no more than wheat is godly or morally good in itself), we can say that it is a reflection of thoughts which are a part of the trend away from God, His values and His character.

Interestingly, there are other views which parallel this idea that we are losing touch with the language of the gospel in creation. Some people take the view that the Industrial Revolution served much the same purpose as atonality - but in this case, it removed people from the daily contact with nature which had always been a part of their lives - rural occupations, "cottage industries", farming, and generally living "close to the land". The advent of mechanization and urbanisation cut millions of people off from close contact with the natural creation. Today, the distortion of the gospel truths inherent in creation is possible in a new way, through genetic engineering, so that perhaps even the "language of the gospel" embodied in the propagation of plants and the cycle of nature may eventually be dispensed with. Whatever the case, the removal of the elements and processes in creation which are "reminders of God" is something that occurs again and again, and is symptomatic of "the trend away from God", man's desire for independence from God and His laws, and the satanic desire to remove every trace of the gospel from the world.

Natural Harmony

Another way of looking at the tonality issue is to argue that atonality distorts the order and pattern inherent in harmony as found in nature, in the laws of physics, and as expressed within the tonal language. There is certainly an obvious sense in which some notes blend and others don't (in tonality, the terms are "consonance" and "dissonance").

The false medieval theory of "diabolus in musica", discussed in chapter 2, was born out of this concept.

The physical laws of "natural harmony" are most easily explained by examining how the notes of a sounding string are produced. The horizontal lines in Fig. 1a represent a string such as a guitar or violin string; the short vertical lines represent divisions of the string length where it is "stopped" by a finger. Thus **1** in Fig. 1a is the whole string; **2** is the string stopped at the halfway point; **3** is the string stopped one third of the way along, and so on.

Fig. 1a

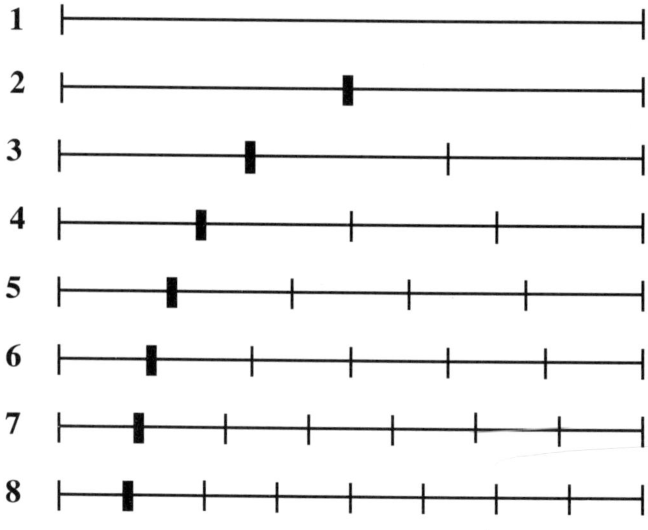

Fig. 1b shows the notes produced from these "stoppings" of the string in mathematically precise divisions.

Fig. 1b

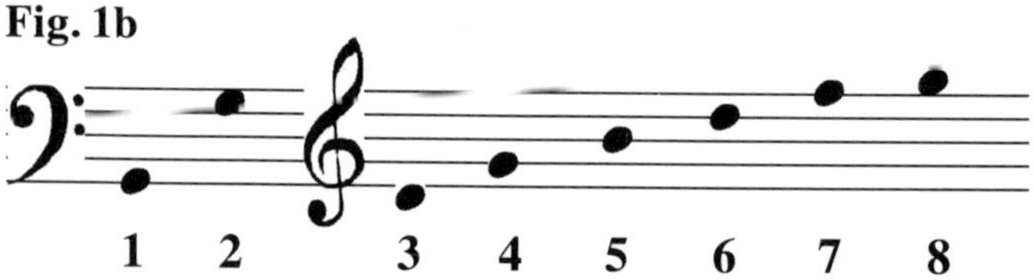

In this example we are assuming that the whole string produces the note **G** (the first note in Fig. 1b, numbered **1**). When the string is stopped at the halfway point (**2** in Fig. 1a) it produces the note numbered **2** in Fig. 1b - exactly one octave above the note for the whole string length. Mathematically precise also means musically precise!

It would follow logically from this that the note produced by stopping the string one quarter of the way along would produce a note exactly two octaves higher than the full length string - which it does.

Stopping the string at the one third mark yields a note exactly one octave and a fifth above the whole string note (note **3** in Fig. 1b corresponding to length **3** in Fig. 1a). Lengths **5**, **6**, **7** and **8** in Fig. 1a correspond to notes **5**, **6**, **7** and **8** in Fig. 1b. All these notes are in precise numerical ratios to each other.

Moreover, the note of the full-length string is actually not just one note at all, but a whole "chord" of notes above the basic "fundamental". This is true of all musical notes (excepting pure electronically produced sounds generated for oscillators and similar equipment). The "fundamental" is the note we hear, because it is the loudest and clearest. However, many of the other notes (known as "partials" or "overtones") are also audible to the trained ear. These overtones turn out to be exactly the same series as are obtained from dividing the string into half, thirds, quarters, and so on! The overtones contained in one fundamental note are exactly the same notes shown in Fig. 1a. Thus for the fundamental note **G** (numbered **1** in Fig 1a), the 1st overtone is **G** one octave higher (numbered **2**) - exactly the same note produced by stopping the string halfway along its length (**2** in Fig. 1b). The second overtone, **D** (**3**) is the same note as is obtained by stopping the string at the one-third mark; and so on, with each overtone existing in a precise mathematical relationship both to the fundamental note and to the string length.

These overtones also constitute the basis of tonality. In fact, the first four overtones of a "fundamental" constitute the notes of the major chord belonging to that fundamental note (Fig. 2).

Fig. 2

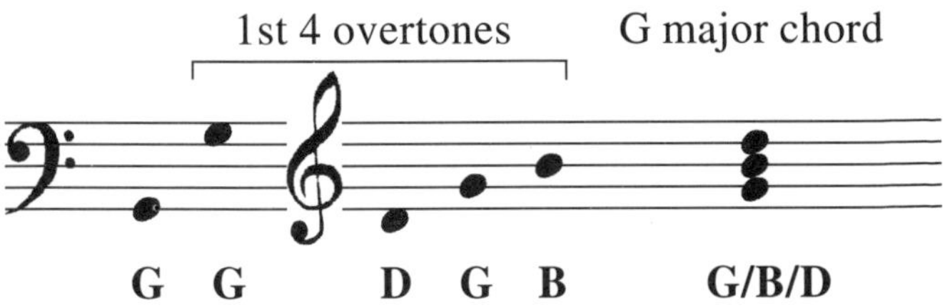

The dividing of notes into the 12-semitone octave is also based on these naturally occurring overtones. So the relationship between tonality, naturally occurring "harmony" and mathematics is very clear. Order and pattern occur in all of nature, and this too seems to be a godly principle; therefore it is reasonable to conclude that any distortion of it is in some sense a perversion of that principle. As we have seen, there are New Age theories which attempt to tie up these principles of harmonic order with the patterns created by the relationships of the planets, and this is all seen as evidence for pantheism (the idea that God is everything and everything is God). But in the end these theories fall down, and the pattern and order in the universe and in music serve better to illustrate the existence of a personal Creator than they do to support New Age concepts.

Perverting God's Order

When we examine the commandments God gave to Moses, we find that things that pervert the natural order are actually grievous sins in God's eyes. There are many prohibitions and injunctions in the Law of Moses; but only a few times is something said to be an "abomination" to God. Amongst these "abominations" are the sins which pervert, confuse or mix up the natural order of things: homosexuality and bestiality, for example (Lev 18:22-23), which pervert the natural sexual pattern of man and woman; or for a man to wear women's clothes, and *vice versa* (Deut 22:5). All these are called by God "abomination". Similar injunctions (though without the status of "abomination") are found in Deut 22:9-11: an ox and ass should not plough together; a garment should not be made of mixed materials (e.g. wool and linen); a vineyard should not be sown with mixed seed, "lest the fruit be defiled". In each case, it is the mixture and confusion of the natural order that is wrong in God's eyes.

Things that distort or pervert creation are actually tantamount to blasphemy against God, because creation reflects His character; therefore to pervert the order of creation is to slander God's character. As Christians we are called to reflect God's character in our lives and in everything we do. It seems reasonable to suggest that as we progress and mature in the Christian life we should become more aware of the things that reflect God's character and glorify Him, and also more aware of things that present a distorted or perverted image of His character. Discernment in every area of life ought to be one of the prime and distinctive marks of the Christian. Without it we are prey to "seducing spirits and doctrines of demons" (1 Tim 4:1) and a thousand other subtle twists and counterfeits. Our warfare consists in standing against such things; but to stand against them, we need to be aware of them.

Alex Robertson has been part of Barratt Ministries since 1985. Trained as a classical musician, his ministry includes music, Bible teaching and writing.

He is available for meetings and seminars on the use and abuse of music and other subjects of relevance to Christians today. For more information, please contact Barratt Ministries at the address below.

For a full list of Barratt Ministries publications, including teaching cassettes, music albums, videos and tracts, or to join the mailing list for "Challenge", Barratt Ministries' free bi-monthly teaching articles, please write, phone or fax:

Barratt Ministries
Manchester M14 5QH
England
Tel & Fax: (44) (0)161 224 2620

BMP